37
UNIROYAL
TOWALL TRAILERS

LOTUS SEVEN

Graham Arnold

CONTENTS

ISBN 0 85429 385 X

A FOULIS Motoring Book

First published 1984

Published by:
Haynes Publishing Group
Sparkford, Yeovil,
Somerset BA22 7JJ

Distributed in USA by:
Haynes Publications Inc.
861 Lawrence Drive, Newbury Park, California 91320, USA

Editor: Rod Grainger
Dust jacket design: Rowland Smith
Page Layout: Anne Wildey
Colour photographs: Majority by Andrew Morland, taken especially for this book.
Road tests: Courtesy of *Motor* and *Sports Car & Lotus Owner*
Printed in England by: J.H.Haynes & Co. Ltd

Titles in the *Super Profile* series

Ariel Square Four (F388)
BMW R69 & R69S (F387)
BSA Bantam (F333)
Honda CB750 sohc (F351)
MV Agusta America (F334)
Norton Commando (F335)
Sunbeam S7 & S8 (F363)
Triumph Trident (F352)
Triumph Thunderbird (F353)

AC/Ford/Shelby Cobra (F381)
Austin-Healey 'Frogeye' Sprite (F343)
Corvette Stingray 63-67 (F432)
Ferrari 250GTO (F308)
Fiat X1/9 (F341)
Ford GT40 (F332)
Jaguar E-Type (F370)
Jaguar D-Type & XKSS (F371)
Jaguar Mk 2 Saloons (F307)
Jaguar SS90 & SS100 (F372)
Lancia Stratos (F340)
Lotus Elan (F330)
Lotus Seven (F385)
MGB (F305)
MG Midget & Austin-Healey Sprite (except 'Frogeye') (F344)
Morris Minor M.M. Series (F412)
Morris Minor & 1000 (ohv) (F331)
Porsche 911 Carrera (F311)
Rolls-Royce Corniche (F411)
Triumph Stag (F342)

B29 Superfortress (F339)
Boeing 707 (F356)
Harrier (F357)
Mosquito (F422)
P51 Mustang (F423)
Phantom II (F376)
Sea King (F377)
Super Etendard (F378)
Tiger Moth (F421)

Further titles in this series will be published at regular intervals. For information on new titles please contact your bookseller or write to the publisher.

FOREWORD

Fashions in cars change with the years, but sometimes one car is able to stay through more than one fashion. The Seven is such a car and all but the purists would say that the Seven has been in production for so long that it is now, in the Caterham version, really a replica of itself!

The Lotus Seven was introduced originally for the impecunious enthusiast who wanted to beat both Purchase-Tax and fellow car enthusiasts. It has now become the cult possession of people who can, and frequently do, afford several other more comfortable means of transport. It combines the rugged outdoor life of a motorcycle and sidecar with water-proofing standards only slightly better than could be provided by a sieve. It imparts unending exhilaration and enjoyment to its owner .... even when it doesn't go!

This book was much harder to write than my sister volume on the Lotus Elan, because the Seven has never been 'understood' outside of the Lotus company. It was built and sold to 'pay the rent' and keep people in jobs when the production of racing cars, by Lotus Components, was at a low ebb, i.e. in the summer when everybody wanted a 2-seater sportscar and everyone who was anyone had taken delivery of a new Lotus F3 or Formula Ford around mid-January. It did *not* benefit from any continuous engineering input, least of all from Colin himself. It only had intense marketing and promotion when its natural sales level dropped and we needed the money. Despite being ignored and even abused by Lotus it became strong, like the first born males of Sparta, and survives as a cult car to this day.

In my last Super Profile I forgot to thank the owners who put up with me and my Taiwanese tape recorder so in this book they are top of the list. I would also like to thank all those who let us photograph their cars at the first ever national gathering of Seven owners at Beaulieu in 1983. People to be named by name are first of all Graham Nearn of Caterham Cars Limited with whom I spent many hours playing " ... and do you remember when Colin did this and that .....?", before we got down to details. Also Roy Badcock who, as Joint General Manager of Lotus Components Limited, 'lived' almost every Seven made until he took over Twin Cam engine production at Lotus Hethel in 1967. Then there are those members of Club Lotus who at some time in the past sent me a photograph of their car – and now they see it in this book. I apologise for not giving you a mention by name but hope that your car will now go up in value because it can be advertised as 'Featured in Seven Super Profile'!

I must thank 'Tinker Bell' my secretary. Because I can't remember names (and hers is Wendy) I knew it was something to do with Peter Pan and that it wasn't Captain Hook or the Crocodile so she became Tinker Bell. Wendy typed the first manuscript as therapy as her husband died in the same week as Colin Chapman in 1982.

My final thanks are to my flock of geese – when things weren't going right I would go and talk to them and throw some slices of bread. Their stupid looks soon sent me back to the typewriter!

Graham Arnold

HISTORY

Ancestry and influences

In postwar years, the design of tubular chassis became the same exact science as had been the case for the Barnes-Wallis-created Wellington Bomber and R100 Airship. The favourite phrase was "triangulation", even amongst those who did not know what they were talking about. The ultimate spaceframe of the period was probably the 'bird-cage' Maserati which was beloved by all who saw it, but by none whose job it was to bend it straight after an accident or replace its mechanicals.

Colin Chapman's first essay into stressed tubular construction could be seen in his successful 750cc Mark 3 racing two-seater, although the vehicle still retained the original Austin Seven chassis, as laid down in the regulations. The Mark 6 was the first pure Chapman spaceframe, light in weight, incredibly rigid and easy to work on.

The Lotus 6

Just as the Lotus 6 was descended almost directly from the successful Mk 3 with its 750cc Austin 7 side-valve engine, so the Seven came via the Mk 6.

The first 'production car' produced by Lotus Engineering, the Mk 6 featured an advanced (for its day) spaceframe chassis designed to take mainly Ford 10 parts.

The Mk 6 was actually designed and built-up from a mass of detailed calculations which included stress analysis at a time when other firms were still working on the basis of "we'll need another tube in there ..." Using body panels hand-shaped by Williams & Pritchard, the car was designed to take a variety of contemporary engines up to 1500cc, including Ford Consul, Ford 1172, MG and even Coventry-Climax. In races the Lotus "giant killing" capabilities were now extended beyond 750 Motor Club short distance events and many owners of cars costing up to ten times as much as a Lotus 6 were soundly beaten. Although more than 100 of these "indecently fast" cars were built and sold, they are a rare collector's item today. And, as we know, they can still put up winning performances as instanced by Chris Smith's immaculate car illustrated elsewhere in this book.

It was the Mark 6 which put Lotus into the car manufacturing business, but the Lotus Seven widened the marque's appeal, creating the foundation for all those Elites, Elans, Europas and the modern-day cars that keep the Lotus name up front in every way.

Concept of the Seven

The concept of the Lotus Seven envisaged an ultra-light car which would give open-air motoring fun with considerable competition potential at club level. There was to be minimal provision for weather protection and the carrying of luggage – factors in keeping with the lightweight philosophy.

When the Seven was first conceived, the engines available had only a modest power output, so aerodynamics were not an important factor in the design as the car could not reach high enough speeds for it to become significant. Also, it was Chapman's claim for a long time that effective aerodynamics were receiving excessive amounts of attention when other aspects of vehicle design could contribute much more to overall performance.

The car's outstanding mid-range road performance was to be achieved through favourable power-to-weight ratio and superb handling, Chapman already being acknowledged as a genius at designing cars to out-corner almost everything else irrespective of price.

The roads and tracks of the world have witnessed numerous examples of Sevens out-performing, out-handling and out-manoeuvring cars costing much more and producing more than twice the power. Designed from the outset to be sold in kit form, the Seven was sufficiently versatile to accommodate a wide variety of engines from a humble side-valve 1172cc Ford unit through to a 'one-off' fitment of turbo-charged Lotus 16-valve 2.2-litre, Rover V8 and, of course, in the USA a wide and wild variety of American V8s.

B.Sc. (Eng.) may have been the formal qualification that enabled Colin Chapman to pen so many of his brilliant designs; combined with his post-graduate training in structures with British Aluminium and his own 10/10ths style of driving. This experience gave rise to the design of a chassis incorporating round and square-sectioned tubes of various diameters. Every significant load and deflection had been calculated, and provided for, in the overall design: yet the chassis weighed just half a hundredweight!

Whereas the Lotus Mark 6 featured an ingenious conversion of a Ford beam axle by the skilled use of a hacksaw for the front suspension, Colin adopted fully independent suspension with rack and pinion steering for the Seven, incorporating the same front suspension components which were to be seen on the Elite Climax and early Formula 2 cars. The Seven featured distinctive and steeply-cambered combined spring and shock absorber front suspension units, which were to become so much the hallmark of this famous model.

With so few predecessors in the Lotus line-up, the influences on the Seven's concept are to be found in the cars against which it was intended to compete. These were mainly based on the pre-war approach, with very firm suspension giving a hard ride. The shortcomings of these vehicles – excessive weight, high frontal area, poor handling and indifferent adhesion – enabled Colin Chapman to draw up his design objectives. The total Chapman philosophy called for a car which was light in weight, adequately powered, had suspension which kept the wheels upright with a long, progressively-damped suspension movement and a high degree of rigidity and compliance in the chassis suspension.

Production prototypes

Although Lotus Engineering did manufacture a prototype Seven, the Mark 6 was really the basis for the development of the later car. Testing of the first Seven was therefore confined to journeys to and from Chapman's home, and early races.

For the Seven, production of Lotus chassis moved from the Progress Chassis Company at Edmonton (headed by ex-Lotus employee, John Teychenne) to Arch Motors, who have been associated with the car ever since. The metal body panels were produced by Williams & Pritchard in Edmonton, and the quality of their workmanship is still evident in those early cars wherever they appear. The amount of Lotus involvement in the actual building of the Sevens was minimal, in that the cars were almost always sold in kit form so that Lotus Storeman (later Purchasing Director), John Standen, only had to ensure that the kits were fitted with some basic equipment and trim before being delivered to, or collected by, the customer. The fact that many of these kits had bits missing and double rations of others is all part of the Lotus legend!

Although reported many times before, it is worth remembering that Colin Chapman was in the forefront of those specialist car manufacturers who discovered a chink in the armour of the purchase-tax laws and turned it into an industry. At the time, purchase-tax was levied on all new cars, but not on car parts. Colin Chapman, and other manufacturers, discovered that if a customer purchased the components for his car in kit form, from just two separate paper companies under the same roof, the car did not have to carry punitive purchase-tax. This was just another example of Colin Chapman's life-long fascination with the legal bending of regulations to his own advantage.

Development philosophy

Talking to those who worked at Hornsey when the Mk I Lotus Seven was being built, one quickly realises that it was constructed in the true Chapman tradition of the day – build it and run it! The first car was literally built from sketches and that was it!

Development, especially that for the Mk II, was not only aimed at improved performance, improved durability and even improved handling, but also at getting the cost of component production down and adding a little more sales appeal. Any resulting improvement in the power to weight ratio of the Mk II was a profitable bonus. Even future developments to allow the car to take different axles and engines had more to do with cessation of supply rather than a real desire to improve the car. Normally a great impetus to improved car design, official regulations were ignored, with the exception that the original cycle-type mudguards had to be replaced by the more stylish (and legal for America) later fitments.

Original Sevens met the then current clubman regulations for racing, and just about stayed within the Construction & Use Regulations laid down under British law. From its earliest days, the Seven has caused nightmares for overseas distributors and much head scratching for bureaucrats. "Zee doors do not meet zee regulations", says an official. "But it has no doors", replies the prospective importer! "Zen it is illegal", says the aforementioned official.

Development of weatherproofing was almost ignored at the factory, although Lotus accounts employee, Warren King, recalls how he fitted sidescreens to his car in his spare time so professionally that the factory copied them and offered sidescreens as an extra! Such things as heaters were fitted by the owners until the factory realised the profit potential of these items, but total waterproofing and real weather protection – NEVER! A solution to the US demisting requirements was seriously suggested at one time – offer Brooklands aeroscreens only!

The Lotus Seven caused Colin Chapman to coin one of his famous, and very wise, statements and that was: "all cars put on weight". Slowly the Series I increased in weight from 8cwt to 9cwt, until Chapman determined that the weight should come down again, even though it was planned to make available lighter and more powerful engines. Chapman's argument was that if you could take 50lb weight out of the car and put 20 more horsepower in it, it would go a great deal faster than a car that put on 20lb whilst receiving the benefit of 20 horsepower, *and* material costs would be reduced!

A careful reappraisal of the over-engineered and over-triangulated Lotus Seven Series I chassis was therefore carried out and it was decided that in the absence of any known common areas of fatigue failure, many of the original tubes could come out. With hindsight it is now considered by experts that the chassis was rendered a little too flexible, especially in the scuttle area, and only today have Caterham Cars really put back all of the stiffness and rigidity which was essential to achieve the best handling, especially with more powerful engines. Although much of the development road testing was done by Lotus Seven customers, albeit unknowingly, Chapman used to take the occasional car for commuting, and as a result recommended some modifications or improvements.

Changes to the cars were very infrequent on explicit orders from Chapman who 'fought' his own employees throughout his life. "I've only got to go away for a few days and they'd alter every car we make," he once told the author, "so anyone who alters a car without my written permission gets the sack!"

It would be wrong to extend too much of the Chapman aura to later Sevens as he would have been the first to admit that they were a profitable left-over from earlier days. He was never seen to drive one at any time from 1962 until 1971, except for a quick run round the Lotus test track in a Series IV. He had said that a logical replacement would have three wheels and a modern motorcycle engine, but the back wheel would be as wide as the front wheel of a mdern F1 car. Chapman never admired his own handiwork once it had been bettered by another of his brilliant designs, and he once said of his collection of significant Lotus cars: "The day I start restoring that lot I will no longer be able to think about the future – I sometimes wonder what came over me when I look back at some of my ideas".

Colin always said that he designed all his cars (and later luxury motor yachts) for his own requirements *at that time.* Hence we went from the Seven to the Elite, then, via the Elan, to the Plus Two while the Europa was succeeded by the Esprit as the Elite and Eclat took over from the earlier 2 + 2s.

Development highlights

During the life of the Series 1 Chapman's abject dislike of Burman steering saw the introduction of the Triumph Herald rack and pinion unit which continued into the Series 2, introduced in mid 1968.

The Series 2 car contained some typically Chapman efforts at cost reduction rationalised, at the time, as improvements. The spaceframe was lightened by removing several tubes, the nose cone was replaced by a cheaper, better-styled glassfibre moulding, along with glassfibre rear mudguards. The American-market full length front mudguards were supplied in glassfibre and these were so well styled that the public demanded them on the UK cars as well.

The Series 2 also followed automotive fashion of the sixties, adopting 13 inch wheels, whilst the option of spoked wires was deleted. Drum brakes were retained and the iniquitous 'A' bracket appeared on the rear suspension. The original engine range available for the Series 1 was very substantially augmented by the introduction of Cosworth modified 109E 1340cc units in addition to the standard Ford engine. These were later followed by the new Ford 1500cc 5-bearing crank engines in standard and Cosworth form. By 1961 Seven prices had not increased significantly from the previous models, and this reflected the then low rate of inflation in the UK. In those days heaters were optional and of the fug-stirrer type.

The demands of the American market both for touring versions of the Seven and cars eligible for S.C.C.A. competition were probably the biggest single influence on the development of the car. What the Americans called the 'clam shell' front mudguards were dictated by American market requirements and it is amusing by today's standards to note that it was not until the introduction of the Series 2 that windscreen wipers became standard equipment. This was at a a time when many Ford and Austin-based specials had vacuum-operated windscreen wipers that stopped at full throttle! It was perhaps in the choice of engine capacity, and specification, that the American competition demands had the most influence, and it is unfortunate that in the end an excessive American preoccupation with legislation made the Lotus Seven illegal in the USA for many years.

In 1968 under new management Lotus Components decided to revamp their image and this called for a re-launch of the Lotus Seven as sales were dropping badly and the proposed Series 4 was behind schedule and still had not been approved by Colin Chapman.

The Series 3 was intended to feature some beefing-up of the chassis tubes in several areas: but there was a problem in raising the extra cash to have the jigs modified and a large number of old-style chassis were already in stock at the Hethel factory. The biggest change was the dropping of the Triumph rear axle in favour of the Ford Escort unit. This was because Triumph axles had, at last, ceased to be available. To enable the same wheel to be fitted front and rear (Ford pcd) new front hubs were also introduced at this time. The 'price leader' version of the Seven was available with 1300cc Escort engine (225E) and Cortina 116E gearbox but this specification was rarely, if ever, ordered. The mainstay was to be the Ford 225E 1600cc crossflow Ford engine in Cortina GT trim.

At about this time the rush to build Formula Ford racing cars for the new and very popular Formula fell flat on its face, and Lotus Components had almost 100 unsold units in stock. (Caterham came to the rescue later and bought the majority as part of the Licence to Manufacture deal). Lotus Components had entered into a very binding contract with Holbay for blue-printed engines, so the Lotus Seven was an obvious recipient. As a result the Super Seven S was introduced using this FF engine complete with twin Webers, 4-branch exhaust, etc. In a cash flow crisis engines were actually removed from Formula Fords and reworked for the Seven line! The customers were no doubt delighted!

While, over the years very, little changed in terms of chassis, suspension and creature comforts the Seven did 'grow up' as better engines, tyres, brakes and gearboxes appeared giving greater performance *and* better profit margins.

Throughout his life Colin Chapman enjoyed a close relationship with Ford and even considered a takeover offer in 1964. One of his favoured ex-directors, Mike Costin, had left with Keith Duckworth to form Cosworth and supply Lotus with Formula Junior engines based on the 105E. The name Cosworth had appeal so Chapman was more than happy to offer the 1340cc 3-bearing 109E engine from the Ford Classic in Cosworth form as an option. It was light, powerful and came with a four-speed all synchromesh gearbox at a very low price. This relationship with Cosworth eventually blossomed into the Cosworth DFV Grand Prix engine via the four-cylinder Formula 2 unit. It also cost Lotus their Twin Cam business in later years. Ford adopted the Cosworth 16-valve design for their RS1600 replacement for the Escort Twin Cam.

During the early 60s disc brakes were coming down in price to car manufacturers and Lotus had been amongst the early users in racing. It was therefore a natural step to add disc brakes as an option on the front of the Lotus Seven once Lotus could see a worthwhile profit from the fitment. Colin frequently opposed adding new items to cars if this could not maintain his profit ratios which were stated quite simply as: *Materials + labour x 2.8 = retail price.*

The Series 2 cars also became available on Dunlop SP tyres as radials came down in price and Chapman's Team Lotus associations with Dunlop were strengthened. The author must stress once again that the Seven was not developed as a result of market research or a purist desire to incorporate all that was best in automobile design. It had to sell to pay the rent, and a major proportion of the wages! Myths should not be permitted to develop in this area – the Seven was frequently ignored, neglected, dropped and resurrected as needs dictated – Lotus just didn't tell anyone. It was scheduled for extinction at several board meetings but survived because nobody got round to carrying out the execution, or a big order appeared in the post ...

The advent of the Series 4 was not the sales disaster now suggested by those who would decry the car. Around 1000 units *were* sold and they are owned and loved wherever sports cars are driven. As mentioned elsewhere the car was a whole new vehicle based on what the Lotus directors felt was the next logical step forward. They may yet be proved right. No kit car builder today could come up with a vehicle that equals the Series 4 in handling, workmanship or durability. The main mistake was for Lotus to drop the Series 3, but Caterham resolved that situation to their ultimate benefit and not insubstantial profit.

Caterham, when they returned to the Series 3 car, used the chassis specification drawn up for the Twin Cam Super Seven. This stiffened up the bulkhead, engine bay, transmission tunnel and steering rack mounts. They also adopted the Ford 2000E gearbox with a variety of engines including the Vegantune-produced Lotus Twin Cam, Cortina GT crossflow, Holbay 1700 Sprint and the later Vegantune VTA Twin Cam with toothed-belt-drive to the camshafts.

As always, a Seven can still be purchased less engine and gearbox and as we go to press Caterham are working on a scheme to enable owners to buy a kit phase by phase, starting with the chassis and then as time and/or money permits they can add suspension, transmission, etc. Such an extended purchase plan can only be adopted on a car that has become a replica of itself in its own lifetime and won't change noticeably between now and the end of the decade, or even perhaps the century.

In the Caterham era popular, fashionable interest in bigger tyres has seen the cars go from narrow 145x13s on 4.5J rims to 185/70HR 13s on 5.5J and some private owners have gone even bigger.

Seven S and SS Twin Cam

With the Lotus Seven Series IV already coming along well as a replacement for the Series III, Lotus Components Limited couldn't let the old model fade away so it was decided to go out on a high note with the S and SS Twin Cam. Both these cars relied almost completely on the Series III mechanicals but the S featured a Holbay-tuned version of the ever-popular Ford Cortina 1600GT engine, while the SS boasted a 125bhp Lotus/Holbay twin cam based on Holbay's F3 experience. Both cars ran twin Webers and chunky 5.5J x 13 wheels with 165 x 13 Dunlop SP tyres to put all that power down and help stop the car when required, although the large contact patches didn't do much for the car's wet weather behaviour! Lotus alloy wheels were also offered; these wheels being about the only remaining sign of a failed Lotus enterprise. Brand Lotus was going to be used to market a wide range of universal car accessories but it just never happened, and stocks of Lotus shoes, anoraks, etc, remained unsold.

The SS Twin Cam was effectively one of the first British "limited edition" cars, with its custom interior and metallic silver bodywork and trim. It was stated at the time that only twelve would be built, but chassis numbers 13 and 15 seem to surface from time to time . . . It is also suggested that an "aggrieved" senior executive may have done himself "one for the pot" prior to moving on to better things!

Graham Nearn, of Caterham Cars, has an SS Twin Cam in his "never to be sold" collection. The concept of the Twin Cam was intended to be carried over to the Series IV but Lotus themselves never got round to it, and Caterham effected the transformation of this model.

The Series 4 Seven – Cinderella?

Sales of the Lotus Seven were slipping, and it was no "cult car" at the time Lotus Components Limited, under MD Mike Warner, gazed into their crystal ball and saw mounting losses ahead.

They looked at the cost of construction, they looked at the lack of styling and weather protection and they looked at cars like the Morgan. "Unacceptably expensive to build, unacceptably short of styling and unacceptably short of comfort and weather protection". That was the verdict reached in the mid-60s. Four men, Mike Warner, Alan Barrett, Dave Baldwin and Peter Lucas started to detail a new Seven. In those days Colin Chapman was operating a style of management based on picking the right men and then giving them almost *carte blanche* to make a name for themselves (or ruin the company). It was probably the only style for such an itinerant Chairman to adopt until "Management by Objectives" was brought in during 1969.

Main internal changes to the Series 4 were to be found at the front end, where the suspension had been borrowed from the Lotus Europa, whilst the rack & pinion unit was by Burman. The rear axle was still rigid, but taken from the Ford Escort (as was the Series 3) with the addition of Watts linkages and radius arms eliminating the old full-width A-bracket. The chassis was still tubular, but more rigid at the cost of some increase in weight.

The all new styling of the Series 4 was neat and functional with the use of a glassfibre body, a proper hood, and sidescreens with sliding perspex "windows". As a car it is without doubt a practical, clean and very competent design. As a Lotus Seven replacement it just didn't work.

The Series 4 was offered with the 84bhp Ford crossflow 1600cc GT engine, or an uprated version by Holbay (part of a contractual obligation to buy a lot of Formula Ford engines) or, eventually, the Twin Cam 1558cc engine.

As a Director of Lotus at the time, the author would like to put right some misconceptions as to Colin Chapman's involvement with the Series 4. After he had fallen out with the then Managing Director of Lotus Components Ltd, Mike Warner, Colin was reported as saying that he had never seen the Series 4 before it was announced. He was in fact a very regular and ebullient visitor to the workshop in which Dave Baldwin and Alan Barrett were building the prototype, and all those involved with the project could possibly take the blame for the decision to supersede the Series 3 with a car which seemed at the time to be the correct replacement.

The Caterham era

After years of trying, Lotus enthusiast Graham Nearn of Caterham Cars Limited eventually obtained Chapman's signature and a handshake on a deal that would allow him to keep the Seven going for many years to come. Having closed down Lotus Components Limited, Chapman was happy to see the Seven continue in production as the Caterham Seven. Initially this deal was aimed at keeping the Series 4 going, but Graham soon detected a groundswell of demand for the departed Series 3.

Unknown to many, Caterham have very substantially re-engineered the cars to improve their handling and durability as well as making sure they meet at least most of the regulations in their main markets including the UK. The new "long cockpit" version is just one example, another of which they are naturally proud is their joint development of the latest Caterham-Vegantune VTA engined Twin Cam model which is selling well at home and abroad.

A new engine had to be developed when Lotus withdrew the original Twin Cam in the face of possible product liability claims in overseas markets, hence the VTA. Caterham Cars Limited build new

Caterham Sevens to order, supply a complete parts and service backup to all Sevens, including Lotus originals, and usually have a mouth-watering stock of well presented used models in stock at their Town End, Caterham Hill premises, South of London.

Caterham's chassis are built for them by long-established specialists, Arch Motors. The Caterham specification differs from that of Lotus by fuller triangulation in the engine bay. Also the front bulkhead and scuttle have been strengthened and extra rigidity built into the steering rack mounting areas. Finally, a steel tube integral gearbox mounting strengthens the floor and tunnel area. All this stiffens up the chassis without adding an unacceptable increase in weight.

Today's Caterham can be hard to distinguish from the original Lotus Seven. The increased height of the nose and engine cover will almost certainly go without comment and by reverting to the original toggle switches, Caterham will have pleased the traditionalists whilst the long cockpit version will enable more portly customers to enjoy the thrills of Seven ownership. Only engineers will detect the dual system brakes with front discs, 6 inch alloy wheels, stronger Escort 2000 axle and a general tidy up of electrics, plumbing, etc. 90% of the continuous engineering development carried out by Caterham on the Caterham has been well and truly "under the skin".

In October 1983, Caterham announced that the German authorities (TUF) had given the Seven full certification, thus opening up a very lucrative market that will soon include other European countries.

As sole worldwide licensees for the continued production of the Lotus Seven, Caterham Cars Limited have noted the regular introduction of replica 'Sevens' which infringe their rights. In addition to any legal action that they may take, Caterham stress that such cars are *not* Type Approved or recognised in any way by the leading clubs catering for the Seven owner.

Some special Sevens

Throughout the years various individuals and specialists, and the factory themselves, have turned their attentions to "one-off" versions of the Lotus Seven. Peter Kirwan-Taylor, joint designer of the Lotus Elite and still a Lotus Director, put a very attractive streamlined body on an early Seven. The factory produced a "one-off" Lotus "Seven A" with independent rear suspension based on the Lotus Elite rear end, and this special won the Clubman Championship driven by then-Lotus U.K. Sales Manager, John Berry.

Some years later Lotus Components Limited produced another "one-off" all-independent car to be driven by Tim Goss. This car, under the designation "Seven X", was also very successful in Clubman racing.

Probably the best of the Seven specials is the "Black Brick", a racing car which earns for itself a separate section in this book.

Various owners have carried out engine transplants. The fitting of a standard Lotus 907 16-valve 2-litre engine is one example; a Lotus 7, in the final stages of preparation, and fitted with a turbo-charged Esprit engine(!), is another.

Graham Nearn introduced the Silver Jubilee Seven to celebrate twenty-five years of Seven production. It was silver, as one might have guessed, and offered a very superior standard of trim, with leather seats, and many highly polished metal components. Each car had a special commemorative plate on the facia.

Black Bricks

The glory and the glamour of the Lotus Seven would be incomplete without mention of Rob Cox-Allison's "Black Bricks". For the few who don't know, Rob is the owner of a chain of Home Centres called DESIGN, and his sport is racing very fast versions of the Seven.

His first car featured Formula 2 front suspension and an 1800cc Twin Cam. This Seven got its name because it was black, and has the aerodynamic efficiency of a brick. The next car had Chevron front suspension and could be used with a 410B Hart Formula 2 engine, where the regulations permitted. The same car ran with an 1800cc Twin Cam in ModSport events, sometimes being converted overnight to race in different events just 24 hours apart. The rear wheels were a massive 14 inches wide to get the power down onto the track, over 300hp of it in the case of the Hart engine! Aerodynamic aids consisted of ground-effect side pods, front spoiler, biplane-type wing and, of course, the hood was always up.

Black Brick III does not attempt to be all things to all classes, as it is specifically for ModSport events. The latest Brick has an 1800cc Racing Fabrications Twin Cam giving around 200bhp. Cars like Black Brick keep the Lotus Seven mythology alive.

The Whiting sprint and drag Seven

The car featured on the cover of this book is James Whiting's magnificent sprint and drag Caterham Seven Twin Cam. The car has a 165bhp 1600 Twin Cam engine running on twin 45 DCOEs. Cosworth L.1 cams are used in conjunction with Powermax pistons giving 10:1 compression. 'Mike the

Pipe' from Wallington produced the 4-branch exhaust and ignition is Piranha. An AVO 'Rocket' gearbox gets its power through a twinplate competition clutch. A limited slip 4.1:1 or 3.9:1 Escort Twin Cam axle puts it all on the tarmac.

The front suspension is of James' own design, and is chrome-plated to show standards. It is of wishbone and rose joint configuration and fully adjustable. The Compomotive 10 inch rims with Goodyear slicks can be seen through wire gauze let into the front wings. This enables the car to retain the flared wings of the original without any of the usual aerodynamic penalties.

The car has turned 0-60 in 4.7 seconds with a 5th wheel and under 13 seconds for the quarter mile. James has a lot of plans to improve the car so these details are probably history by now. We thank him and everyone else who provided their cars for photography.

The Antipodean Seven

Down in New Zealand the Lotus importer is offering a stretched version of the Seven Series IV complete with 2.2-litre Lotus 16-valve engine and 5-speed gearbox. The Steel Brothers Seven 907 is made at PO BOX 11-077 Sockburn, Christchurch, NZ.

Return of the 'Seven-A'

Avon Coachworks, famous for their upmarket versions of the Lotus Sunbeam have also worked their magic on the Caterham Seven to give us the 'Seven-A'. The specification adds a little luxury in the form of carpeting, heat-proofing of the passenger's footwell plus two tone paint, special wheels and a modified hood. Customers have a wide variety of fittings to choose from so each job is done on a custom basis at an agreed price.

The DSK Turbo Seven

DSK Engineering of Marblehead, Massachusetts, USA, used to specialise in parts for the Lotus and Caterham Seven. Now they have taken the plunge and offer their own turbocharged replica. They redesigned the original chassis to provide even greater strength to accept the torque of a turbocharged engine based on the Ford Pinto unit. Turbocharging gives the car a top speed similar to the Caterham VTA or Sprint.

Vegantune in the Caterham story

Vegantune of Cradge Bank near Spalding, Lincolnshire were already established tuners and re-manufacturers of Lotus Twin Cam engines before they put the Lotus Twin Cam engine, using the taller 1600 crossflow (Kent) block with a new front cover, back into production for the Caterham Seven.

This was done with initial blessing from Lotus but, subsequently, this approval was withdrawn as a cautionary measure due to possible legal complications associated with product liability laws. Vegantune therefore decided to produce their own engine. In doing so they designed out most of the original shortcomings of the Lotus engine, and created a new Twin Cam head mated to the Ford "Kent" 1600cc 5-bearing bottom end. The new engine which resulted featured belt-driven camshafts, water cooled exhaust valves, a choice of inlet manifolds and greatly improved oil circulation.

Designed from the outset to be turbocharged, the Vegantune VTA Twin Cam produces 195bhp in turbocharged form and around 140 bhp, with twin Dellorto carburettors, when placed in the Caterham Seven. Vegantune still rebuild and re-manufacture original Lotus Twin Cam engines as well as producing the VTA for Caterham and other customers. Currently a big-bore VTA is planned for selected export markets.

Engines in the Lotus Seven

As with the Lotus 6, Colin Chapman designed the Seven with a variety of engines in mind. The engine bay is quite generous in width and height despite the low line of the bonnet. Most four-cylinder units up to 1600cc can be accommodated and only the Coventry Climax unit was ever inclined at an angle.

A large number of Seven kits were sold 'less engine and gearbox' as the owner either had his own units or planned to experiment.

In the original design concept discussions at Hornsey, and in the pub next door, Colin stressed the importance of designing a car to have one engine and gearbox unit from the same manufacturer. 'This eliminates the cost and bother of mating a Ford engine to an MG gearbox', he would say, no doubt remembering what had gone into fitting various gearboxes to the sidevalve Ford 100E 1172 engine which came with a three speed box as standard in the Ford Anglia and Prefect.

The original Mk 1 series cars could be made to accept the 1172cc Ford engine which was required in the 'Clubman 1172' class of racing, a BMC A-series 948cc engine from the A35 (single carburettor) or Sprite (twin SUs) or the rich buyer could go for the Coventry Climax 1100cc with the BMC A-series gearbox and Speedwell gears. Even the BMC B-type unit from the bigger Austin saloon could be fitted. This latter fitment was developed on a semi-private basis by Graham Hill when he was working at Hornsey on gearbox assembly in exchange for an occasional drive.

Some owners of the earlier

Mk 6 transferred their engines, so one or two MG 1.5-litre XPAG units found their way into early Mk 1 sevens along with at least one four-cylinder 1700cc Ford Consul unit.

The following is a summary of engines offered. Most of these could be purchased in standard trim or with the benefit of the performance conversions offered by famous names of the day like Aquaplane, Speedwell, Cosworth, Holbay, etc.

Ford 1172cc side valve 100E.
BMC (Austin/Morris) 948cc overhead valve A-series unit.
BMC (Austin-Healey Sprite) 948cc overhead valve A-series unit.
Coventry Climax 1097cc overhead camshaft, all aluminium FWA.
Ford 105E 997cc overhead valve.
Ford 109E 1340cc overhead valve.
Ford Cosworth 1340cc overhead valve.
Ford 1498cc overhead valve (5-bearing crank).
Ford Cosworth 1498cc overhead valve (5-bearing crank).
Lotus Ford 1498cc twincam.
Lotus Ford 1498cc big valve twincam.
Ford 1599cc overhead valve.
Lotus Ford 1599cc (tall block) twincam.
Holbay Ford 1599cc overhead valve.
Vegantune Ford VTA 1599cc tooth belt-operated twincam.
Holbay Ford 1700 'Sprint'.

Axles in the Seven

As mentioned elsewhere in this publication, the first three Lotus Seven chassis were built to accommodate a version of the de Dion rear suspension used in the Lotus XI. The first true production Mk 1 with its 1172cc Ford sidevalve engine featured a version of the BMC A-series rear axle as used in the Austin-manufactured Nash Metropolitan with a 4.8:1 final drive ratio. This axle was wider than that used on the A30/35 giving the car a rear track of 3ft 10 ins. This was a hypoid bevel unit with optional ratios of 5.375, 5.125, 4.55, 4.22, 3.89 and 3.73. The axle casing was modified to provide mounting points for the combined coil springs and damper units which made up the suspension and for the pick-ups for the parallel trailing arms and Panhard rod.

Approximately 12 months after the car was introduced supplies of rear axles dried up so Lotus turned to the Standard 10 axle as fitted to the Triumph Pennant or Companion Estate car. This took the rear track out to 4ft 0½in. The normal axle ratio was 4.5:1. A 3.9:1 or 4.1:1 was also available from among others in the Standard Triumph range. The introduction of the Pennant axle saw the elimination of the Panhard rod, an A-bracket layout being adopted. The amount of power fed through these axles by later, larger, engines soon caused problems but Lotus turned a blind eye to them. The trouble was caused by the casings cracking and losing all their lubricant. These cars had the Triumph Herald nosepiece in the standard casing with a 4.1:1 ratio. The Lotus factory demonstrator 8843 AR, probably the most powerful version, often had a new axle on Monday after a busy weekend of sales demonstrations from the Cheshunt factory! The addition of strengthening plates had almost eliminated this problem in the hands of private owners.

With the Triumph 10 range out of production, Lotus joined the scramble to buy up remaining axle stocks from dealers while Lotus designers set about finding an alternative: the problem was the narrow track of the Seven when compared to contemporary saloons.

The total lack of aerodynamic considerations in the Seven's design, unless the screen was removed, meant that higher axle ratios did nothing for the top speed. The cars just came up against a solid wall at just over 100 mph and it took a lot of extra power to break through the 110 barrier. It was a brave man who checked his speedo reading at around 100 mph as the instrument was on the far side of the facia in a frighten-the-passengers position. The best axle ratio for power up to 80 bhp was 4.1:1 or less. With Cosworth Power, 3.9:1 combined with the optional close ratio gearbox gave optimum performance. Today's cars offer 3.7:1 or 4.1:1.

After 1965 Triumph deleted the drain plug from their axle casing. This was in line with the development of 'infinite life' axle oils. A cracked casing would soon rectify this omission!

Looking through the Ford parts bin Lotus identified the potential of the Ford Escort rear axle which would give a wider track of 4ft 4 in. In Seven form the axle had a modified casing with bracketry for the trailing links and dampers and the A-bracket under the differential. This, however, was a *different* type of A-bracket not interchangeable with earlier models. The Ford axle was used with a 3.7:1 ratio but Ford's Special Vehicles Department supplied Ford Sport dealers with a wide variety of alternatives including limited slip variants. This axle and hardier derivatives from the RS range became common to all Sevens, including the Series IV until the early eighties when Caterham moved to the Ital unit. This robust axle is 28lb lighter than the Ford and had also resolved a problem with wheel hubs. S3 Sevens use Spitfire front uprights with hub adaptors to enable the car to use Ford pcd wheels front and rear. Now Triumph pcds are used in conjunction with different wheels. Ratio Options are 4.1:1 or 3.7:1.

Selling the Seven

Lotus adopted various formulae for

selling their cars at home and abroad during the in-house production of the Seven. Initially, the home market was covered by Lotus Centres who received a commission on every car sold. It had to be done this way to keep the Purchase Tax people happy. Then with stocks of unsold cars building up, Chapman increased his direct selling activities in 1961 and while slashing the kit price substantially reduced dealer margins to just £20. Advertising at that time accentuated how easy it was to build a Seven from kit form in less than 48 hours.

The main promotional effort was based on obtaining the maximum number of rave road tests using several specially prepared press cars, and the car registered 8843 AR in particular. For a while this had the ex-Jo Siffert Formula 1 Cosworth-Ford engine (without its dry sump) and it certainly impressed the press and broke a few axles!

In the United States several distribution arrangements had ended in liquidation and so Chapman went over himself to rescue both the road cars and production racing cars. He signed up several new distributors and two of them were given the exclusive rights to New York! As he said afterwards to Ron Richardson, export sales manager, "They'll never find out!" The stronger of the two, Peter Pulver, then went on to put Lotus really on its feet in the Eastern area of the United States and proved very successful with his own Seven in the SCCA races. Pulver also masterminded each year's SCCA submissions from Lotus to get the best classification as, in a badly organised year, the Sevens could find themselves matched with 7-litre Shelby Cobras, whilst only permitted one carburettor!

Meanwhile, on the American West Coast, Bob Chalman of Ecurie Shirlee Corporation, Los Angeles, was doing well for Chapman and for the Seven.

Back at home, Caterham Cars had managed to obtain the exclusive concession to sell the Seven and retained this right despite some rather political in-fighting amongst Lotus directors in the late 1960s. As a result Caterham continued to build the car under licence, but were not allowed to call it a Lotus. Today Caterham hold the worldwide distribution and product support rights, with all other versions of the Seven dubbed as spurious or even forgery!

Graham Nearn considers that sales of the Seven are a barometer of prosperity. When the stock markets are booming he has a long waiting list and when the economy goes into general decline demand drops away. Although they have never had to build cars for stock, sales did drop away in the worst of the depression of the early 1980s, after boom sales in the expansionist 1960s and through part of the 1970s.

Caterham admit that the weird TV series *The Prisoner,* which featured Patrick McGoohan and a Seven, has done a lot to make a cult car out of the Seven. McGoohan originally contacted the author at Lotus asking: "Do you make the sports car that has pop-up headlamps? We want one for a TV film." As the Elan was then featuring in *The Avengers* we took both an Elan and a Seven (KAR 120C) to which we had added metal headlamp guards, for McGoohan's appraisal. McGoohan looked at the two cars and said "I'll have that one", pointing at the Seven. It was that easy – *and* we got it back after the filming was over!

Lotus Seven advertising was always minimal at home and abroad and the brochures were a fine example of Chapman's dedication to lightweight products – although they now change hands for substantial sums in autojumble sales. One Seven advertisement of the 60s suggested to all benevolent fathers that if they bought their young sons toy trains for Christmas when they were six (so that they could play with them themselves) they should now be thinking along the lines of a Seven for a seventeen year old! One very catchy advertisement featured an oarsman getting out of his boat with a very pretty girl standing by to greet him; the slogan? "Out of an eight, into a Seven and carry one".

Racing a Seven

Just as many famous racing car designers including Colin Chapman, Eric Broadley and Len Terry had served their apprenticeships in the Austin 7 based 750 formula, so aspiring racing drivers could be seen competing for victory in the 1172 Clubman Formula. The Lotus Seven, like its predecessor the Six, was designed to compete in this formula and was successful for more than 12 years. Up to the mid-60s a Seven owner could prepare his car at home, drive it to the circuit at weekends complete with tools, sandwiches and girlfriend, race and then drive home with his trophy!

Such well known Grand Prix drivers and international track stars as Graham Hill, Peter Gethin, Patrick Depailler, Piers Courage, Derek Bell and Peter Warr of Team Lotus campaigned Lotus Sevens in their early days. Sad to relate, the simplistic structure of club racing was upset by Lotus themselves when their own Sales Manager, John Berry, ran away with the championship in the Lotus 37 known as the '3-7' in 1965. This car put the clock back to 1957 when the first three Lotus Seven Mk 1 prototypes featured de Dion rear suspension and other pure racing features. The 3-7 had a fully independent rear suspension, dry sump Cosworth 1500 engine and, in the words of a contemporary employee at Lotus Components, "we put all we knew into that car". It subsequently passed from Berry to Peter Deal, to Tim Goss. It then disappeared into Lotus Components Limited and the Lotus Seven X appeared to take the Clubman Championship yet again. This frantic activity had been occasioned by the arrival of the Chevron Clubman which was reputedly based on Brabham F3 suspension. Subsequently, Mike Warner of Lotus took the car into the Development Department yet again where it grew Lotus 41X Formula 3 suspension from the car tested and race developed by John Miles (X stood for 'Experimental' and was a marketing ploy which was supposed to say to customers "If it works we will put it into next year's production cars"). The car was always closely pursued and even beaten by privately prepared Seven-based cars, most of them reverting to the old-fashioned cycle type front mudguards.

Lotus involvement ended when Lotus Components Limited, (re-named Lotus Racing), was put into liquidation by Colin Chapman – so ending an era. The 7X was further developed into the 7Y, still using F3 experience; Y follows X! The Lotus 7Y then went on to more success but the fat was in the fire. The British Racing & Sports Car Club voted to ban the Seven and Graham Nearn of Caterham Cars started his battle to get the car reinstated while such exotic creations as the Black Brick and Dave Bettinson's cars were campaigned in more enlightened championships.

Author's Note: There may have been 'rule book' reasons why the 3-7 kept its original identity: there are those ex-employees who will claim that an all-new car was in fact built around the original chassis plate. Alternatively, Lotus wanted to help the owner without letting him know just how much help they were giving!

THE CLIMAX/DE DION SEVENS: The prototype Seven Mk 1, with its front suspension taken from the Lotus 12, was loaned to longstanding Lotus customer Edward Lewis for hillclimbs and speed trials, before the 1172 Ford engined car had even been made public/ With typical Chapmanesque duplicity Colin affirmed that there would be no variations on the basic Seven and that the Lewis car had just been an overpowered development hack to test components! Then when two customers appeared, cheque books at the ready, two more de Dion chassis, and two more sets of wire wheels and disc brakes were found at the back of the stores! Jack Richards and Paul Fletcher were happy men indeed.

Preparing your Seven for racing

Before investing any money in the preparation of your car it is essential to make a careful study of the various classes, competitions and championships available to you, the programme involved and the approximate cost of participating. In Britain it would be essential to obtain the *RAC British Motor Sport Year Book* from the RAC Motor Sports Association Ltd, 31 Belgrave Square, London SW1. In other countries one would obviously contact the equivalent organisers or motorsport governing body. Caterham Cars should also be able to advise. Vehicle specification regulations for every type of RAC-approved competition are clearly laid down in the *Year Book* and these should be studied carefully, assuming you decide to use a modified Seven in a class which does not permit dramatic alterations away from the original specification.

SAFETY: Your first consideration should be personal safety. This calls for the fitment of a strong roll cage combined with full-harness safety belt including crutch strap, the mandatory external ignition cut-off switch and static or automatic fire extinguishers. Very careful attention should be paid to fuel tank mounting and fuel lines, adopting aircraft quality materials (Aeroquip) wherever possible. Your personal involvement with survival should obviously extend to the very best crash helmet and flameproof driver's kit.

IMPROVING THE HANDLING: After all aspects of safety have been taken care of you should look to improving the handling of the car within the regulations. This calls for reference to modifications carried out by successful Seven drivers in the same class and by talking to Caterham Cars themselves. Today's successful Seven features the widest possible, most expensive tyres available fitted to the best quality lightweight alloy rims within the regulations.

Competition quality fully adjustable shock absorbers will be mated to harder or softer springs and stiffer or more flexible anti-rollbars as a result of extensive track testing on circuits to be visited during the season. The car will also benefit from the fitting of a higher geared steering rack, although substantial improvement derives from using a smaller competition quality steering wheel.

Although most new arrivals on the racing scene feel that they should start off with the most powerful engine available, your author recommends as much attention as possible to improved handling, improved braking (harder pads and linings) and very great concentration on driver skill and consistency. It is sometimes better investment to enrol at a racing drivers' school than to drop a 'demon' engine under the bonnet!

ENGINE PROTECTION: When we finally come to the tuning of the engine there are three vital essentials to long engine life, unless you can afford rebuilds between meetings!

1) Adequate engine

lubrication: This calls for the fitment of a flexibly mounted oil cooler in a non-vulnerable position in an area which benefits from copious quantities of fast-moving cool air at all speeds. The oil cooler should be connected to the engine oil pump via aircraft quality flexible piping. The oil selected should be racing quality from a major manufacturer, preferably one of the latest synthetics. Oil additives are not recommended by major manufacturers. The oil cooler will also increase your car's sump capacity and you should take advice from engine tuners on the need to fit some baffles to avoid oil surge, and therefore bearing starvation, during cornering. A truly accurate, well-positioned, pressure gauge is obviously essential.

2) Cooling: The car's radiator hoses and waterways must be in good condition, free of obstructions and capable of withstanding the pressure marked on the swirl pot filler cap. The cooling system should be filled with top quality aluminium corrosion-inhibited anti-freeze and, of course, a top quality, easily visible water temperature gauge is essential.

3) Engine balance: So many enthusiasts start their quest for increased power with camshafts, carburettors, etc. which all increase the strain on the bottom end. Your author recommends a fully-balanced bottom end with top quality bearings followed by the power-increasing addition.

ENGINE TUNING & GOOD AERODYNAMICS: In terms of power increase per pound invested, the following is the best order of investment for drivers planning to race a Lotus Seven, assuming that turbo-charging is outside the regulations and that the regulations have been studied very carefully in all respects.

1) A Carburettor choke for every cylinder: Two twin choke sidedraught carbs (Weber or Dellorto) will give the best possible power output on a professionally designed manifold. Engines over 1600cc will benefit from the larger (45 series) Weber.

2) 4-branch racing exhaust system: A free-flowing 'bunch of bananas' exhaust manifold, venting through the minimum legal silencer system, is an essential to achieve increased power.

3) Camshafts: A clear understanding of what performance you require is essential when selecting camshafts for a racing engine, and this is related to choice of axle ratios. For hillclimbs and long-distance events a camshaft producing high torque may prove very successful and provide greater engine durability than some peaky high lift unit. Cosworth, Vegantune, Piper, Holbay, Q.E.D., Burton – the list of camshaft specialists is very lengthy and can be obtained through any of the performance-orientated motoring magazines. It should be remembered that the fitment of a camshaft with substantially different characteristics from the original calls for alterations to the chokes and jets on the carburettors and to the advance characteristics of the distributor. Selection of final settings, including valve timing, where adjustable, should take place on a dynometer or at least a rolling road.

4) Headwork: Attention to the cylinder head, racing compressions, modifying combustion chambers, fitting larger valves, opening up the ports, gas flowing and all the other magical technology offered by the top quality engine preparation companies can be expensive and usually provides the least improvement for the money invested.

5) Aerodynamics: When the car is turning competitive times, with reliability and real consistency, further improvements can be brought about by attention to the fitment of rear wings, air dams and even side skirts.

With all the above modifications, the true effectiveness of your investment can only be evaluated by continuous track testing on specific track testing days. Testing is different from practice: it should be noted that all the successful teams only change one significant aspect of the vehicle during each five or more laps of testing, *i.e.* changing tyre pressures to induce over-steer. The effect of this on a stopwatch will not be known if at the same time you vary the shock absorbers, fit a large rear wing and alter the distributor!

Testing is tedious and needs a consistent driver before any true conclusions can be drawn.

The author would like to express once again that total compliance with the regulations is essential, as fellow competitors will be quick to protest your car if it is successful, especially if they can see, or have reason to believe, that it is 'bent'.

A Caterham Seven *can* be raced with very minor modifications in a wide variety of competitive events in the UK. Graham Nearn's advice to newcomers to the sport is 'Work Your Way Up', *ie* get the most out of yourself and a standard car before investing in a programme of improvements.

And what of the future?

As mentioned earlier in this book, the Seven has become a replica of itself over more than a quarter of a century. Caterham Cars know what makes this car sell so we won't see any alterations or modifications that change its visual appeal. Independent rear end perhaps, more powerful engines of less than 2-litres perhaps, slight improvements in the aerodynamics perhaps, but, like the play *The Mousetrap,* the Seven will go on playing to packed audiences right into the 21st century.

A seven is still a car to appreciate both in financial and fun motoring terms – I wish I still had one!

Some Seven eccentricities

ONE EYED? The very early Sevens had a strange, and now illegal Lucas headlamp arrangement provided by what were really just spot/foglamps, as sold by Halfords. The nearside headlamp had a wide beam and the off side a pencil beam. On encountering a car coming in the opposite direction the intrepid Seven driver flicked his 'dip' switch, which projected out of the facia, and off went the offside headlamp!

BOILERS. Early Lotus Sevens had no cooling fan fitted, mainly because there was no room and Mr. Kenlow had not yet made his mark with the electric alternative which was optional on later models. Any driver of an early Seven would do almost anything to avoid getting stuck in a traffic jam in August! The addition of a swirl pot helped cooling via the Thermo-Syphon effect in later models.

SWIRL POTS. Many a Lotus Seven owner has wondered at the fabricated 'tin can' into which he has to pour water if the coolant level is low. It sits at the front of the engine and has the radiator filler cap on top. This is a 'swirl pot', as seen on many racing cars. It creates a high point in the cooling system as the normal header tank down in the nose is lower than the highest point on the block. As its name implies it creates swirl in the cooling system, eliminates air locks and is an essential part of the car. Do not remove it!

GUESS THE FUEL CONTENTS. Under the quarter tonneau, concealing the sparse hood, many a Seven owner had a simple calibrated stick. This was his petrol gauge! It was many years before real gauges became standard on the Seven.

BURNT LEGS AND RHEUMATIC ELBOWS. Unwary passengers entering or leaving a Lotus Seven often have the scars to show for their carelessness, as the exhaust silencer runs alongside the car's bodywork and gets very hot. The exhaust tailpipe comes out at ankle height so enthusiastic owners soon discover that it is possible to scorch the stockings off pretty girls at bus stops!

Because there is no room for the driver's right elbow inside the car, earlier cycle wing cars soaked this unfortunate part of the anatomy as soon as it started to rain. As a result Lotus elbow became a well-known affliction – and windscreen wipers were required on the driver's glasses!

GETTING IN (AND OUT). Getting in and out of a Seven with the hood up is a difficult manoeuvre and, for the author (20 stone), impossible! Getting in, one has to stretch the left leg deep down into the car whilst bending the right leg as far as an accomplished limbo dancer. Then, by leaning the torso well back, it is just possible to insert oneself. Getting out usually involves putting the palm of the right hand onto the pavement!

RAPE HANDBRAKE. Many a lady passenger in a Seven feared a fate worse than death when the driver's hand lunged down between her legs. But the innocent driver was only reaching for the handbrake!

How many are there?

In addition to the practice of "one for the pot" adopted at Hornsey in the early days, Lotus' chassis numbering system and subsequent claims have a greater place in *Alice in Wonderland* than any other publication. From the best figures available, including those from chassis suppliers we get the following:

Series I:	251.
Series II:	1362.
Series III:	385
Series IV:	887.
Caterham:	Figures for Caterham Series 3 and Series 4 not revealed. Estimated at around 2000 at the time of publication.

EVOLUTION & SPECIFICATION

Series 1

Chassis Nos 400 to 499
Chassis Nos 750 to 892
1957 up to August 1960
Approx 250 cars built and sold
* Later nos represent Cheshunt built cars.

Chassis Space frame triangulated multi-tubular incorporating stressed skin alloy reinforcement via undertray, side panels and propellor shaft tunnel. Bodywork in aluminium, fully detachable bonnet. Cycle type front wings. Full width windscreen. Detachable hood and tonneau listed as options. "Chip Cutter" grille in nose. No visible air intake on bonnet. Silencer alongside passenger seat venting at 45 degrees to rear/side, ahead of rear wheel. All cars right-hand drive ex-factory.

Suspension Independent at front, incorporating fabricated lower wishbone, combined coil spring and shock absorber with anti-roll bar. Rigid rear axle with Panhard rod and trailing arms; coil and damper suspension. Steering (on approximately the first 50 cars) Burman worm and nut, replaced by rack and pinion. Wheels 15 inch pressed steel 4 inch rims. Dunlop spoked wheels and splined hubs optional.* Brakes 8 x 1½ inch hydraulic drum front and rear.
*Wire wheels standard on Climax powered cars.

Engines For further engine details see separate panel.
Basic LOTUS SEVEN (F). Ford 100E side valve 1172cc with Ford 3-speed gearbox (synchro on second and third only). Options included Aquaplane modified cylinder head, twin SUs and fabricated exhaust. Also BMC A-series 4-speed gearbox. Options also included hub caps, spare wheel, windscreen wiper, hood and tonneau. Export model had above as standard.
SUPER SEVEN or (SEVEN C). Fitted Coventry Climax FWA SOHC aluminium engine with A-type 4-speed gearbox. Later models had optional B-type gearbox with close ratios (see text). Wire wheels and splined hubs standard.
SEVEN AMERICA (A). BMC A-type engine and gearbox. Full length front wings as adopted on all later models. Flashing indicators front and rear. Side screens, spare wheels, rev counter, cooling fan, soft top, tonneau and floor-covering. The British Seven (A) featured the BMC A-series engine in a car to the same specification as the (F) with options available as listed.

Series 2

Chassis No 1004 to 2101
October 1960 to June 1968 approx. 1370 cars built and sold.

Chassis Cost cutting version of Series 1 chassis featured less tubes and reduced weight. Side panels, nose and wings built in glassfibre. Revised nose line. Full length front wings available on all models for all markets. Wire mesh in nose. Soft top incorporated extra transparent panel to improve rear quarter vision. Spare wheel and windscreen wipers now standard equipment. Side screens listed as options. Heater available.

Suspension Steering rack position changed to make left-hand and right-hand drive cars available – now ahead of wheel centres. 13 inch wheels on Triumph Herald pcd. Wheel width rose during production run from $3\frac{1}{2}$J to $5\frac{1}{2}$J. Wire wheel option deleted. A-bracket introduced to replace Panhard rod on rear axle.

Engine For further engine details see separate panel.
SEVEN (F). Same as Mk 1 specification
SEVEN (A). 1098cc BMC A-series engine offered in addition to the 948cc. Twin SUs and 3-branch exhaust. Sprite 4-speed gearbox.
SEVEN AMERICA. BMC 948 or 1098cc engines to 'Sprite' specification to meet SCCA regulations. Twin SUs, raised compression, 3-branch exhaust. A-series Sprite ratio 4-speed gearbox.
1961 Ford Anglia 105E engine option offered although customers could still order BMC engined cars if required. 997cc, 48bhp. SUs or Webers. 4 branch exhaust. 4-speed all synchromesh 105E gearbox. This model known as the Lotus Seven A. 'America' name now dropped.
1961 Ford 109E Classic engine added in the SUPER SEVEN COSWORTH 109E. This engine was the same as the 105E but with a longer stroke. Cosworth modified cylinder head, camshaft and exhaust manifold with twin Weber 40 DCOEs on aluminium inlet manifold. 'Cosworth' on ribbed rocker cover. SCCA version for racing in USA had higher compression. Gearbox 4-speed all synchromesh 109E 'Classic'.
1962 SUPER SEVEN 1500. Ford 116E Cortina engine with 5-bearing crankshaft to Cortina GT spec with single twin-choke Weber 40 DCOE and Cortina 4-speed all synchromesh gearbox. First official offering of disc brakes – $9\frac{1}{2}$ inch Girlings on front. $5\frac{1}{2}$J steel wheels with Dunlop SP tyres, now an option.
SUPER SEVEN COSWORTH. As above but fitted with Cosworth modified engine featuring reworked cylinder head, camshaft and exhaust with 2 Weber 40 DCOEs. 'Cosworth' on ribbed rocker cover. Option close ratio gears as used in the Elan.

Series 3

1968 to 1970. Chassis No 2102 onwards. Numbers started with SB and SC for Twin Cam. L on chassis plate means left hand drive.
Approximately 350 cars built and sold.

Chassis As for Series 2 but Lotus added alternative mountings for exhaust and silencer system running full length of car. Later chassis incorporated stronger tubing to stiffen up the rear trailing arm pick-up points and improve front end torsional rigidity. Very last cars had rack height raised to eliminate bump steer. Rear wings wider to accommodate wider rear track. Visual points – bonnet now featured air inlet louvres or scoop depending on engine specification. Silencer still beneath passenger's left elbow but shrouded with slotted heat shield. Exhaust tail pipe vents at rear of car. Dash panel featured rocker switches and fuel gauge. Seat belt anchorages as standard. Winkers front and rear. Fuel tank now filled via external filler cap not through floor of luggage area as previously.
Rear axle now Ford Escort with Escort wheels ($4\frac{1}{2}$J) or Brand Lotus alloy $5\frac{1}{2}$J as options. Brakes 9 inch front disc and 8 x $1\frac{1}{2}$ inch rear drums.

Engines For further details see separate panel.
LOTUS SEVEN SERIES. 3 1300. Escort 1300cc engine to GT spec plus 116E Cortina gearbox.
LOTUS SEVEN SERIES. 3 1600 Ford 225E 1600cc crossflow 4-branch exhaust, Weber downdraft Cortina 116E gearbox.

LOTUS SEVEN TWIN CAM. Lotus Ford 1558cc, 115 bhp. Twin Cam.
LOTUS SEVEN S OR SS. Top of the range cars with 1558cc Holbay Pushrod or Lotus Twin Cam producing 105bhp or Holbay tuned unit giving 125+bhp. (Now a much sought after collector's car). Distinctive 3-piece rear light cluster, special paint and trim, etc.

Series 4

1970 to 1973. At least 1,000 built.

Chassis A 'clean sheet of paper' replacement for the Seven. Tube and ladder chassis with strength added via integral sheet steel side panels. Europa-type front suspension, double wishbone anti-roll bar connected to bottom of shock absorber. Escort rear axle as on Series 3 located by leading and trailing arms plus A-bracket. Rack and pinion steering. 8½ inch disc front brakes and 9 inch drum rear. Front hinged bonnet. Glassfibre bodyshell in four sections. Rigid side screens with horizontal sliding panels for ventilation etc. Hood rear quarter panels can be removed for extra ventilation. Wheels as on Series 3 including Brand Lotus alloy. Rear axle Ford Escort with Escort 4½J or Brand Lotus alloy 5½J optional.

Engine For further details see separate panel.
Same model names as the Series 3 except that 'Super' and 'Twin Cam' were held back for possible later model. Twin Cam engine was not fitted by Lotus to this model. Gearbox Ford 2000E. Caterham took over production in May 1973.

Caterham Seven

Chassis plate carries prefix CS3/----
1974 onwards. Total number of cars built not disclosed.

Chassis Resuming production of the Lotus Super Seven S3. Caterham adopted a strengthened chassis similar to that used by Lotus for the Twin Cam. Stronger rack mounts, stiffer engine bay, radius arm pickups, transmission tunnel and bulkhead. Optional extras included stainless steel exhaust, oil cooler, adjustable dampers. Silencer on near side with perforated heat shield, larger than original S3.
Bonnet top with "Bubble" air intake denotes 1600GT engine; pancake air filters emerging from off side of engine bay denotes Twin Cam; oval grille air intake denotes Holbay Sprint 1700. Nose badge says Caterham 7 although many have since been changed to Lotus badges by owners.

Suspension No significant changes to suspension. Wheels now 5½J with 165 x 13 tyres. Disc brakes on front 9 inch diameter with 8.0 x 1.5 in rear drums and dual systems, collapsible steering column.
'Jubilee' model announced in 1982 to celebrate 25 years. Silver – 8 built only. 1983 car approved by German TUV. Escort axle gave way to Escort RS and then reinforced Austin Rover Ital unit. Dates and chassis numbers for these running changes are not available. Tyre size increased to 185 x 13 (VR) on later models 1983 onwards. All models known as Caterham Super Seven, Caterham Super Seven Sprint and Caterham Super Seven Twin Cam.

Engine For further details see engine panel.

Performance

The following figures have been averaged from a wide selection of contemporary, published road tests. It should be remembered that Lotus used fo fit press cars with 'selected engines' and that some journalists seem to use 'optimistic' stop watches to record faster times than other members of their profession.

	0-60mph	*Standing ¼ mile*	*Top speed*	*Consumption*
Mk 1 Seven(F) 1172 sidevalve Ford	17.8	20.8	81.0	35.6
Mk 1 Seven (A) 948cc Austin	14.2	19.1	80.2	37.7
Mk 1 Seven (C) 1098cc Climax	8.3	16.1	104.6	31.5
Mk 2 'America' 998cc Ford	13.8	19.0	80.5	38.3
Mk 2 Cosworth 1348cc	7.6	15.8	105.6	23.8
Mk 2 1500	7.7	15.9	102.9	24.6
Mk 3 Twin Cam 1600 SS	6.4	15.1	111.0	25.3
Mk 4 1600 GT	7.5	15.8	103.2	25.6
Caterham VTA 1599	6.1	14.3	113.0	21.6
Caterham Sprint Holbay 1700cc	6.1	14.6	112.3	23.0

The above is only a representative selection of test figures. Readers seeking extra information can study Brooklands Books *Lotus Seven 1957-80* and *Lotus Seven Collection No.1* which reproduce road tests on a wide variety of models from magazines published all over the world.

Engine Specifications

	Ford 100E	*BMC A-Series*	*America BMC Sprite*	*Coventry Climax*	*Ford 105E*	*Cosworth Ford 109E*
Type	Sidevalve	OHV	OHV	SOHC	OHV	OHV
Capacity	1172cc	948cc	948cc	1098cc	997cc	1340cc
Bore	63.5mm	62.94mm	62.94mm	72.4mm	80.96mm	80.96mm
Stroke	92.5mm	76.2mm	76.2mm	66.0mm	48.4mm	65mm
Gross bhp	28	37	43	75	39	80
@ rpm	4,500	4,800	5,200	4,500	5,000	5,800
Max torque	53 lb/ft	50 lb/ft	52 lb/ft	65 lb/ft	52.5 lb/ft	80 lb/ft
@ rpm	2,500	2,500	3,300	4,000	2,700	4,000
Comp. ratio	7.0:1	8.9:1	8.3:1	9.8:1	8.9:1	9.5:1
Carbs	1-D/D Solex	1-S/D SU H2	2-S/D SU H2	2-S/D SU H2	2-S/D SU H2	2-40 DCOE Weber

	Ford 105E	*BMC A-series*	*America BMC Sprite*	*Coventry Climax*	*Ford 100E*	*Cosworth Ford 109 E*
Ex. manifold	S.Downpipe	S.Downpipe	S.Downpipe	4-branch	S.Downpipe	4-branch Ex.
Type of fuel pump	AC Mech. Diaphragm	AC Mech. Diaphragm	AC Mech. Diaphragm	AC Mech. Diaphragm	AC Mech. Diaphragm	AC Mech. Diaphragm
Clutch	SDP 7¼in	SDP 6¼in	SDP6¼in	SDP 7½in	SDP 7¼in	SDP 7½in

	SCCA Cosworth-Ford	*Ford 116E*	*Cosworth-Ford 116E*	**Lotus Ford Big Valve*	*Ford Holbay Sprint*	*Ford Vegantune VTA*
Type	OHV	OHV	OHV	DOHC	OHV	DOHC by toothed belt
Capacity	1340cc	1498cc	1498cc	1558cc	1700cc	1599cc
Bore	80.96mm	81mm	81mm	82.6mm	83.5mm	80.9mm
Stroke	65mm	72.7mm	72.7mm	72.8mm	77.6mm	77.6mm
Gross bhp	85	66	95	125	138	144
@ rpm	5,800	4,600	6,000	6,200	6,000	6,500
Max torque	85 lb/ft	78.5 lb/ft	95 lb/ft	116 lb/ft	121 lb/ft	123 lb/ft
@ rpm	4,000	2,300	4,500	4,500	5,000	5,000
Comp. ratio	10.5:1	8.3:1	9.5:1	9.5:1	10:1	10:1
Carbs	2x40 DCOE Weber	1x40 DCOE Weber	2x40 DCOE Weber	2x40 DCOE Weber	2x40 DCOE Weber	2x40 DHLA Dellorto
Ex. manifold	4-branch	S.Downpipe	4-branch	4-branch	4-branch	4-branch
Type of fuel pump	AC Mech. Diaphragm	AC Mech. Diaphragm	AC Mech. Diaphragm	AC Mech. Diaphragm	AC Mech. Diaphragm	AC Mech. Diaphragm
Clutch	SDP 7¼in	SDP 7¼in	SDP 7¼in	SDP 8¼in	SDP 8¼in	SDP 8in

* From around 1976 Vegantune built the Twin Cam using the 1599cc tall block with modified front water pump casing. Power was the same as the big valve Twin Cam but peaked 500 rpm lower down the range. Other Lotus Ford Twin Cams fitted were the 115bhp Special Equipment engine or the Holbay tubed 125bhp Twin Cam – both in S3 cars or SS. Holbay also supplied their Fast Road (FR) 1500 for the S version of the S3.

ROAD TESTS

a Seven for the Seventies

Michael Bowler and Brian Hatton examine the Series 4 Lotus Seven

Even Colin Chapman described the latest Lotus Seven as the best four-weheeled "bike" in the business. What he thought of the earlier ones went unrecorded apart from the fact that owners need no longer suffer from Lotus elbow—a badly shrunken right arm on your best suit. The story behind the latest Lotus 7, the series 4, is one of sophistication underneath a skin that is still recognisably a Seven, still a component car, still marketed by Caterham Car Sales.

The Seven was due to be dropped back in 1964, but demand continued and the decision was reversed in the same year; over 3000 of these stark two-seats-without-comfort projectiles have been produced since it was introduced in 1957.

Motor has kept in touch with its progress over the years. We tested the first one in 1958 with a mildly tuned 1172 side valve Ford unit and three close ratio gears; it had a maximum speed of 80 mph and reached 60 in 16.2secs. The next, in 1961, followed the introduction of the Super 7 with the long flowing front wings and a twin-Webered 1340 cc Ford Classic unit; maximum 96 mph and 60 in 8.5secs. In 1963 came the 1500 cc Super Seven with even more power and a maximum of 103 mph and 0-60 in 7.7sec.

This progression of increasing power was not matched by increasing passenger comfort; obvious changes had been a better hood with more clear panels, a better facia layout, an extra gallon in the fuel tank, disc brakes and a change from the Standard worm and nut steering to rack and pinion.

Now, for the first time, major changes have been made and the series 4 can reasonably be described as an entirely new, waterproof, comfortable Seven. The chassis is still a spaceframe with square tubes reinforced along most of the side by steel sheet, spot welded to the upper and lower rails; the front suspension uses Lotus Europa components and Burman rack-and-pinion steering. At the back, Ford design has replaced the original BMC A-series axle (using the Twin-Cam Escort axle with its built-in radius arm mounts saves welding brackets half way along the tubes). It is located fore-and-aft by a pair of Watts linkages, the arms from the top of the axle going rearwards and lower arms coming forwards from a welded-on drop-down extension of the normal Escort leaf spring location. The Seven uses coil springs mounted high and operating on a triangulated structure level with the top of the after body. Sideways location used to be via a centrally mounted A-bracket attached to a welded-on flange with the load thus being taken where it wasn't originally meant to be. Now however there is an offset semi-trailing link from the centre to the driver's side effectively making a wide-based trailing arm with the lower radius arm. The sideways loads on the axle are taken through the same point as on the Escort. With such location of the axle, there could be some conflict of arcs as one wheel went over a bump, which would result in the axle casing acting as an anti-roll bar and providing instant oversteer. This conflict is absorbed in particularly compliant bushes at the front of the lower arms.

The body construction is completely shown in the Brian Hatton drawing. The bonnet section, of glass-fibre like the rest, is in one piece and hinges forward to give complete engine accessibility. The centre section is also one piece, moulded together from several bits for bolting to the chassis. The inner section is a complete double-bath running from side to side and up over the transmission tunnel. The body is therefore completely watertight with holes only for pedals and steering column; an outer skin is bonded to this and the whole just drops onto the chassis rails—the tail section also incorporating the rear wings. For the first time the standard Lotus colours—orange, blue or yellow—will be pigmented into the glass-fibre; the cockpit half is black

Motor COPYRIGHT

pigmented.
The fixed seats are very comfortable thigh-grippers and mounting points are provided for full harness safety belts; the pedals are also fixed according to the 5ft 11½in. of the standard SAE dummy who seems to have shortish legs and long arms—the steering column can be adjusted, with a bit of spanner work.

For further water-tightness (there is no plug to let any water out), the sidescreens incorporate sliding windows and mate neatly with the hood, which is a

conventional fabric affair. The sticks are spring loaded to provide even tension despite hood stretch. The long sweep of the front wings continues right into the rear wings, keeping out any spray and also providing complete protection from the hot exhaust system running outside the bodywork at that point.

Other details are evident from the drawings and pictures. There is no doubt that the car as a whole is a very big advance over the previous model and will continue to appeal to many hardy enthusiasts, particularly in America where it is reckoned to be a formidable rival to the VW-based Beach Buggies. Should such requirements be necessary for this type of vehicle the facia is safety designed with rocker switches and the steering column is collapsible; there is also provision for a roll-over bar.

In standard form the Seven comes with steel wheels and the Cortina GT engine and gearbox. It is also available with a Holbay twin-cam power unit with 115 bhp or anything up to 135 bhp. With 115 bhp it is said to reach 50 mph in under five seconds! Inevitably the S4 Seven will be used as a Clubman's Championship car and a suitable Holbay engine is offered; apparently there is no truth in the rumour that the Seven has been updated as part of Lotus' campaign against the F100 cars, which at one time were reckoned to be a threat to the continued success of Clubman racing.

Sleek and low but still a Seven, the mark IV uses a space frame chassis with all glass-fibre panelling.

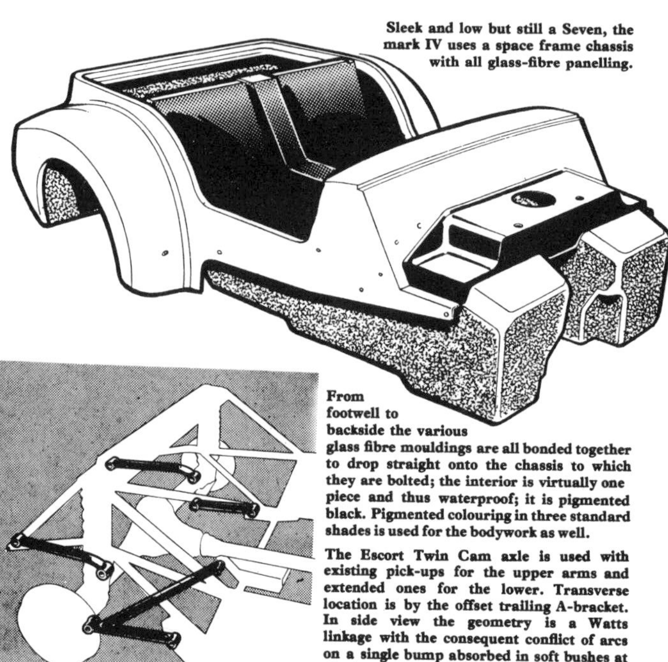

From footwell to backside the various glass fibre mouldings are all bonded together to drop straight onto the chassis to which they are bolted; the interior is virtually one piece and thus waterproof; it is pigmented black. Pigmented colouring in three standard shades is used for the bodywork as well.

The Escort Twin Cam axle is used with existing pick-ups for the upper arms and extended ones for the lower. Transverse location is by the offset trailing A-bracket. In side view the geometry is a Watts linkage with the consequent conflict of arcs on a single bump absorbed in soft bushes at the forward end of the lower arms.

HOW TO BUILD A LOTUS SEVEN

By "Sports Car Fan"

ALTHOUGH there is nothing particularly complicated about assembling a Lotus Seven, many people who have built these cars feel that a guide to procedure would be useful. The set of parts is a little bewildering at first sight, and a great deal of work might be done twice over without a plan to follow. With this in mind I have listed the order of assembly together with the components required.

Before starting to put the car together it is best to take stock of the situation. Before delivery the chassis frame and body unit has been fitted with all the brake piping, brake and clutch master cylinders, dash panel and instruments, switches, regulator and fuse box, starter solenoid, stop lamp switch and wiring loom.

Inside the car are fitted the trim panels, while the rear houses the petrol tank and boot floor. The full width glass screen, body badge and rear lamps complete the external fittings.

You will seen then, that the more exacting jobs have already been done. The next step is to divide the components into their respective sections, and this I will do as we cover each stage of construction.

Having set the car at a working height, making sure that the trestles or beer crates are under a frame member and not merely an aluminium panel, remove the bonnet and nose cowling. Unscrew the boot floor and side trims, which are held with self tapping screws, and the tunnel top and body centre section, which are bolted.

Check that the tapped holes in the chassis are clean and then try the correct bolts for fit, making sure that you smear graphite grease on them first. Nuts, bolts and washers will be listed after the instructions for the fitting of each component. All threads used are U.N.F. unless otherwise stated.

FRONT SUSPENSION AND STEERING

Components
One pair of wishbones fitted with trunnions and kingposts.
One anti roll bar and mounting blocks.
One pair top arms.
Two suspension units.
Eight bonded rubber half bushes (long).
Two hubs, bearings and caps.
One pair steering arms.
One pair brake assemblies.
Two brake drums.
One rack and pinion and clamps.
Two ball joints.
One steering column and mountings.

1. Assemble each side as a unit, and fit the two-leading-shoe brakes to the kingposts. The bottom bolts screw into the steering arms which are fitted so that the track rod end is on top.

Bolts
Four bolts ¾″ x $\frac{5}{16}$″.
Two bolts 1½″ x ⅜″.
Two bolts 1¼″ x ⅜″.
Two lock tabs.
Four $\frac{5}{16}$″ spring washers.

2. Front hubs; make sure that these are perfectly clean. Pack the inside with grease, of the grade shown on the chassis tag, thumb grease well into the conical inner bearing and place in the hubs.

Tap oil seal retainer into position with the flange to the bearing. Note that the felt seal is squashed between the retainer and kingpost face. Slip hub on to stub pin, push in well greased outer cone bearing, D washer and slotted nuts.

When adjusting the bearings, turn the hub as you tighten the nut. When there is no play, back off the adjustment until the hub is quite free to rotate with the slightest rock. The ideal is .005-.020″ at the wheel rim.

ON NO ACCOUNT LEAVE THE BEARINGS TIGHT.

Split pin the nuts and tap home the grease caps. Fit the suspension units to the wishbones making sure that the tubular spacers are pushed into the rubber eye bushes.

Bolts
Two bolts 2″ x ½″.
Two Nyloc nuts.
Four flat washers.

3. Fit the wishbone assemblies using four of the bonded half bushes at the front pick ups.

Bolts
Two bolts 1″ x $\frac{5}{16}$″.
Two spring washers.
Two halfpenny washers.
Two bolts 3½″ x ½″.
Two Nyloc nuts.
Four flat washers.

4. Fit the top arms into the chassis brackets, and the suspension units to the front of the brackets.

Do not forget the tubular spacers in the rubber eye bushes.

Bolts
Two bolts 3¾″ x ½″.
Two Nyloc nuts.
Four flat washers.

5. The anti-roll bar ends are cranked down 4 degrees. It is important that the bar is fitted the correct way up, so that the threaded ends are parallel to the ground when the car is at normal ride level.

Use the four remaining bonded half bushes (long) in the top arm eyes.

Bolts
Two Nyloc nuts ½″.
Two flat washers.

Next the split aluminium mounting blocks are bolted to the front of the chassis.

Bolts
Four bolts 1¾″ x $\frac{5}{16}$″.
Four spring washers.
Four flat washers.

Do not finally tighten bolts through rubber bushes until the car is on its wheels and at the correct ride level. This ensures that the bonded bushes are set at their neutral position and are not pre-stressed.

6. Connect brake hoses to bottom wheel cylinders, sealing with copper washers.

7. Fit the rack and pinion loosely with mounting clamps.

Bolts
Four bolts 2¼″ x ¼″.
Four Nyloc nuts.
Eight flat washers.

Adjust track roughly by eye, making sure that an equal amount of thread is used on both ends.

8. Fit the steering column so that the square bottom bearing is inside the footbox.

Fit the top bearing and, using the bottom bearing as a template, drill the footbox floor.

Fasten with:—
Four bolts ¾″ x $\frac{3}{16}$″.
Five Nyloc nuts.
Ten flat washers.
One bolt 2″ x $\frac{3}{16}$″.

Slip the splined end on to the pinion, noting that the pinch bolt in the universal joint has a particularly long shank.

Turn the rack and pinion up so that the centre universal joint touches the footbox floor; this ensures that the column will not slip off should the pinch bolt come out.

Do not fit the steering wheel until the car is on its wheels and has been tracked. Set the steering in the dead ahead position, check by wheeling the car back and forth, and then fit steering wheel.

This also applies should an alloy steering wheel be fitted, when the aluminium boss must be drilled, using the wheel as a template.

Six countersunk bolts ¾″ x $\frac{3}{16}$″.
Nyloc nuts.
Six flat washers.

LEFT: Method of Assembly for handbrake lever and cable. BELOW: The rear suspension unit mounting rubbers and caps fitted correctly, i.e., two caps and one rubber below, one cap and one rubber above.

REAR SUSPENSION

Components
One rear axle.
One pair top radius arms.
One L.H. bottom radius arm.
One 'A' bracket.
Six bonded rubber half bushes (short).
Two suspension units.

The rear axle must be fitted so that the pinion flange is on the centre line of the tunnel. Adjustment is provided by shim washers between the 'A' bracket and the axle bracket.

The top radius arms curve away from the suspension units and over the axle.

Fit the suspension units with one rubber and two caps below the chassis bracket, and

one rubber and one cap above.

Bolts
Two bolts 1" x 1/2".
Two spring washers.
Two flat washers.

Do not tighten bolts until car is at ride level.

Bolts
Two bolts 2" x 1/2".
Four bolts 4 1/2" x 1/2".
Six Nyloc nuts.
Eight flat washers.
Two bolts 1 3/4" x 3/8".
Two Nyloc nuts.
Four flat washers.
One bolt 1" x 5/16".
One spring washer.
One halfpenny washer.

HANDBRAKE

Components
Handbrake lever.
Handbrake cable.
One barrel.
One Clevis pin.
One split pin.

Bolts
One bolt 2 1/4" x 1/4".
One Nyloc nut.
Two flat washers.

The action is to push the outer cable with the lever.

Run the cable from the axle linkage through the triangular loop in the rear of the tunnel, the centre hole in tunnel gearbox mounting and a slot in the tunnel cover side. Pass the cable through the wire loop by the lever mounting.

With the handbrake lever in position and the slotted barrel placed in the end, run the inner cable through the barrel, which acts as the outer cable stop, and fit the cable and nipple into the square lug on the chassis.

Adjust the brakes by turning the square adjusters on the back plates clockwise until the drum will not turn, and then slacken off until it will revolve freely. Now adjust the handbrake cable.

FUEL LINE

Components
Hose.
Stems and nuts.
'O' clips.

This is run through the gearbox tunnel mounting left hand hole and the triangular loop at the rear. Clip to the undertray at intervals. The 'O' clips are tightened by squeezing each ear with pincers.

PEDALS

Components
One clutch pedal.
One brake pedal.
One throttle pedal.
Two hinges and nuts.

It is necessary to remove the master cvlinder mounting bracket to enable the throttle pedal to enter the footbox. The brake and clutch pedals are quite straightforward; use in clevis ends.

Bolts
Two bolts 1" x 5/16".
Two Nyloc nuts.
Four flat washers.

BRAKES

Fit the front drums and wheels. Adjust the front brakes; each shoe has an adjuster which should be turned clockwise until the wheel locks. Slacken off until the wheel spins freely then repeat on the next shoe.

Check that all brake pipe connections are tight.

Bleed the brakes. It may be necessary to do this two or three times, and providing the expelled fluid is in a clean container it can be used again after allowing the air bubbles to disperse.

Fit the rear wheels and set the car on the ground.

Check that the suspension is working without fouling by bouncing the car up and down. If all is well the engine can now be fitted.

ENGINE AND GEARBOX

Components
Mounting bar.
Gearbox mounting rubber.
Top water pipe.
Bottom water pipe.
Radiator.
Exhaust pipe.
Silencer.
Propshaft.
SU carburetters and 4 branch manifold if required.

Check that oil filter bolt and all drain plugs are tight.

Remove the fan as this is not necessary.

Replace oil pressure switch with 1/8" B.S.P. union body, sealing with a fibre washer.

Check that propshaft fits the gearbox tail shaft spline. Lay propshaft inside the tunnel but do not bolt to the pinion flange.

Fit speedo cable to gearbox. Slip rubber grommet on gearbox tailshaft casing with flat to the top. Lubricate the grommet with soft soap.

It is as well to protect the forward engine bay cross tube with a piece of slit rubber hose before fitting the engine.

Have two 2" x 7/16" bolts ready to slip into the front mountings, and then lift the engine and gearbox into the car.

Fit the tunnel bracket clamp.
Two Nyloc nuts 5/16".
Two flat washers.

Fit the flexible steel oil pipe to the 1/8" B.S.P. union and run the pipe back horizontally to the bulkhead. Drill a 3/8" diameter hole in the bulkhead next to the vertical tunnel tube and fit the pipe, using the thin lock nut. Screw on the conical end of the plastic oil pipe and run up to the oil pressure gauge, where a leather washer is fitted between the flat end of the pipe and the gauge.

Close - up of the front wishbone assemblies and two - leading - shoe brakes.

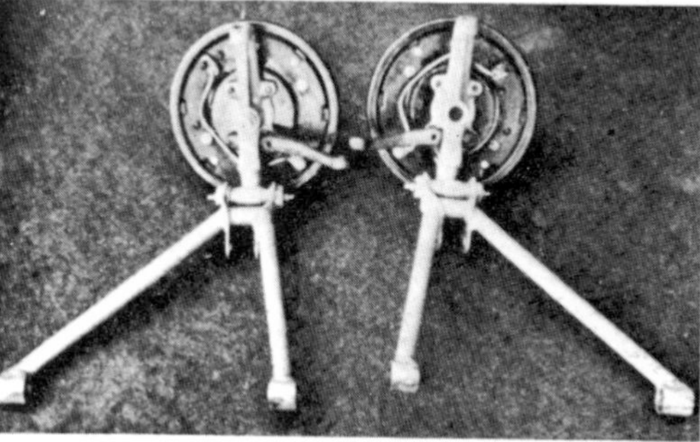

The front wishbones fitted with kingposts and trunnions, steering arms and two-leading-shoe brakes.

Connect speedo cable.

Connect water temperature bulb to cylinder head.

Fit coil.

Bolts
Two bolts 1 3/4" x 1/4".
Two Nyloc nuts.
Four flat washers.

Connect leads to starter, dynamo, coil and distributor.

Fit exhaust pipe, using Ford clamp, to manifold.

Fit silencer to exhaust pipe witn a Jubilee clip.

Bolts
Two bolts 2" x 5/16".
Two spring washers.
Two flat washers

Connect hose to clutch slave cylinder and bleed, using brake fluid.

Note the 4 degree crank of the anti-roll bar end. Both bars are the correct way up.

THROTTLE LINKAGE

Components

One cable.
One cable stop.
One clevis clip.
One pin.
One spring.
One clip.
One bolt 1" x $\frac{3}{16}$"
One Nyloc nut.
One flat washer.

Remove the cranked Solex throttle arm and straighten in a vice. Remove the ball from the arm by filing the burred over end. Refit the arm to the carburetter. Fit the return spring clip to the nearest manifold stud. Replace the existing bolt holding the choke cable clamp with the 1" x $\frac{3}{16}$" bolt.

Fit the cable stop bracket on the bolt and fasten with Nyloc nut and flat washer. Fit clevis clip to throttle arm with pin and fit return spring in pin hole and clip. Fit the cable between the cable stop and throttle pedal arm. The inner cable fits in a bracket on the lower frame member below the arm.

A plate is welded on the throttle arm to act as a return stop; this may need filing to position the pedal.

Fit throttle cable and clips.

TWIN CARBURETTERS

Components

Two SU carburetters H2.
Two stub pipes.
Two gaskets.
Four bolts 1" x $\frac{3}{8}$".
Four Nyloc nuts.
Eight flat washers.
One mounting plate.
Four bolts 1" x $\frac{5}{16}$"
Four Nyloc nuts.
Eight flat washers.
One bonded rubber stud c/w nuts and washers.
One length petrol resisting hose.
Four Jubilee clips.
Two ball joints.
Four $\frac{3}{16}$" plain nuts.
One length $\frac{3}{16}$" studding.
Two spring washers.

Bolt carburetters to mounting plate and line them up with the inlet stubs. Drill a $\frac{1}{4}$" dia hole in line with hole in the chassis bracket.

Temporarily fit the bonded rubber stud, so that the stub pipes and rubber hose can be cut to length. Do not have a greater gap than $\frac{1}{2}$" between the two stub pipe ends.

Fit together with Jubilee clips. Make up throttle link to your liking, using the $\frac{3}{16}$" studding and ball joints.

Cut throttle return spring to size and form end loops. Complete assembly by synchronising both carburetters and fitting the link and spring.

Fit choke cable. Fit side entry distributor cop. Place radiator in position, using the 'top hat' rubber grommets on the mounting pegs. Drill $\frac{1}{4}$" dia hole through the aluminium baffle plate in front of the radiator, using as a guide the lug soldered to the bottom tank.

Bolt together fitting a rubber grommet between the two.

Bolts

One bolt $\frac{3}{4}$" x $\frac{1}{4}$".
One Nyloc nut.
Two flat washers.

The fore and aft position of the radiator is located by the top water pipe.

Bolts

One bolt 2" x $\frac{1}{4}$" UNC.
One bolt $\frac{3}{4}$" x $\frac{1}{4}$" UNC
Two spring washers.
Two flat washers.

Fit bottom water pipe with angle hose to radiator.

Fit the propshaft.

Bolts

Four bolts 1" x $\frac{5}{16}$"
Four Nyloc nuts.

The remote gear control can then be fitted into the tunnel and fastened with
Six bolts $\frac{1}{2}$" x $\frac{3}{16}$".
Six Nyloc nuts.
Six flat washers.
for which you must drill $\frac{3}{16}$" holes in the tunnel sides.

Cut a hole in the tunnel cover for the gear lever. Cut a 3" dia hole in the centre section with a slit to the edge and fit the rubber boot to control rod.

Fit horn.

Bolts

Two bolts $\frac{3}{4}$" x $\frac{3}{16}$".
Two Nyloc nuts.
Four flat washers.

Fit battery.

The suspension bolts can now be tightened.

Set front wheel track to $\frac{1}{8}$" toe in at hub height.

Fit steering wheel.

Fit the front wings and stays with the headlamp mountings to the rear, allowing for full bump clearance inside the wings.

Bolts

Eight bolts $1\frac{1}{4}$" x $\frac{3}{16}$".
Eight Nyloc nuts.
Sixteen flat washers.
Eight bolts, special coach.
Eight plain nuts.
Eight flat washers.

Drill wings for side lamps.

Run wires through wing stays and connect to side lamps.

Fit headlamps, noting that in the dipped position the offside lamp is switched off.

The number plate lamp is mounted on the "D" shaped plate which is in turn bolted to the rear number plate.

Bolts

Two bolts 1" x $\frac{3}{16}$".
Two $\frac{3}{16}$" Nyloc nuts.
Four $\frac{3}{16}$" flat washers.
Two bolts $\frac{1}{2}$" x 5/32"
Two plain nuts.
Two spring washers.

READY FOR THE ROAD

Lubricate all grease nipple points.

Fill engine, gearbox and rear axle with their respective oils.

Fill water system.

Set the tyre pressures to 20 lb sq in front and rear.

On starting the engine check that there is oil pressure, that the dynamo is charging and look for oil and water leaks.

Adjust the carburetter. If you have 2 SUs requiring synchronisation, the Lotus Works will be pleased to provide tuning instructions.

After a short road test check again for leaks.

The running-in speed can be as high as 45 mph in top gear.

When you have completed 500 miles replace all oils and check over nuts and bolts.

The weather proofing can be improved by filling all pop rivets and joints which are subject to wetness with Sealastic or a similar preparation. Obviously it is preferable to do this before assembling the car.

If you plan to paint the car yourself, it is as well to remember to use an etching primer before filler coats and colour.

OWNER'S VIEW

B.J. a City Commodities Broker, aged 43. Lives in Royal Berkshire. He also owns a 1000 cc Honda motorcycle, water-ski-ing speedboat, and an XJ6, and his wife has an Alfa Romeo.

G.A. What first interested you in a Lotus Seven?

B.J. I used to draw them on my blotter at Downside School. I think a Lotus Seven was, and probably still is, every schoolboy's dream – after Dolly Parton!

G.A. What repairs have you carried out?

B.J. Well, as you can see, this is a real Lotus Seven with the 1340cc Cosworth Ford engine and the original Triumph 10 Estate Car back axle. I managed to acquire five of these quite by chance some years ago. The nearest thing we have to a garage in the village hangs in another one every time I split a casing, but I don't do more than 2000 miles a year. Other than that, it is a Lotus isn't it? If it were totally reliable I'd sell it! but I cannot imagine life without the Lotus Seven. The only problem is accommodating my son. He is now 13!

G.A. What do you like most about the car?

B.J. Well, it's ruddy good fun. It is exhilarating, blows away the cobwebs and it certainly turns heads. It really doesn't handle half as well as the pundits would like one to believe. In my opinion, the fastest way to drive it is to imagine it is a Morgan 3-wheeler and drag the back end in whatever direction you want to go.

G.A. What do you dislike about the car?

B.J. Nothing really. Anyone who wants to reduce the noise, stop the leaks and make it warm and cosy has got the wrong car. Perhaps I would like a slightly bigger cockpit, as frequent City lunches seem to have increased my girth over the years!

G.A. What car will you buy next?

B.J. The question does not arise as this car stays in the family forever. If, suddenly, I could not have it any more, I would buy one of those Triking Morgan 3-wheeler replicas being made by an ex-Lotus employee in Norfolk.

It's worth remembering that the late Colin Chapman once said that he would like to design a 3-wheeler using modern technology, and a splendid Japanese motorcycle engine, as a logical continuation of the spirit of the Seven.

G.A. Has your car won any prize?

B.J. No, because I don't own it for any competitive reasons. Mind you, I can always get a Pinta Trophy at my local pub by giving rides!

G.A. What Clubs do you belong to?

B.J. I joined Club Lotus in 1965, and I have been with them ever since. I am in no way a club person but you have got to support the things that Club Lotus does for the marque.

G.A. Is your car in current daily use?

B.J. No, it's not even in monthly use. We have to move the mower and several other items before we can get it out. It is absolutely for high days and holidays. I have used it to go to the office, but by the time I get to the end of the M4 I have got fed up with looking up truck exhaust pipes and been worried about my creased suit!

G.A. What advice would you give to a prospective owner?

B.J. Buy one.

G.A. Have you had any trouble getting parts?

B.J. We have found Caterham Cars, and my little man in the village, capable of obtaining anything we ever wanted. The problem is not getting the parts, it is keeping them in one piece and keeping them screwed in place.

Mr. & Mrs. R.J., live in Peover, Cheshire. Robert is a self-employed Insulation Engineer and his wife runs a Ladies Hairdressing shop; they are both in their mid-twenties.

G.A. What first interested you in a Lotus Seven?

Mrs. R.J. I just told Robert we were going to have one before we got married. My father used to have a motorbike and sidecar, and the greatest treat in the world was to ride beside my Dad. Robert has the Transit for his work and we also have that tatty Mini outside but, as we live over the shop, I don't have to do much driving.

Robert I had always owned bikes until we started courting, but too many of my friends had hurt themselves or their girl friends in accidents, so we decided that it had to be a Lotus Seven. I didn't know anything about Lotus, and I am not sure I do today. I certainly don't follow racing cars, and we take the Seven to Silverstone and Oulton Park to watch big bike racing, not cars.

G.A. What repairs have been carried out?

At this point Mrs. R.J. produced an incredible three-year log of all the repair and service sheets on the car showing that the vehicle had required nothing more serious than a clutch, four tyres, attention to the brakes and several changes of dynamo bracket. The car concerned was one of the last supplied by Lotus Components in 1971, complete with Twin Cam engine.

Robert: We got most of our parts and service from Christopher Neils in Northwich. They are very good, although sometimes their enthusiasm runs away with them.

We took the car to Scotland last year and our only problem was a broken chassis tube which we had welded in Perth.
G.A. What do you like most about the car?
Robert It's got everything that a bike can offer, with safety and, of course, you can carry on an almost normal conversation. I get enormous enjoyment out of leaving almost every other make of car ever made away from the lights. It is quite incredible what it does to Porsche and other very expensive cars. I used to do this with my motorcycle, and it is something that gives me the greatest satisfaction.
Mrs. R.J. It's so funny! Some fellow looks down on you from his big Mercedes, in his dark glasses and toupee, and when the lights go green we've gone! It is also incredibly 'nippy', quite economical and just a lot of fun.
G.A. What do you dislike about the car?
Robert The damn Police Traffic Patrols. It is quite impossible to drive the car in this area, by day or by night, without getting a 'pull'. It really has become our biggest single source of aggravation. We don't have any endorsements, we have a full insurance No Claims bonus and yet the Police can never leave us alone. We even got stopped half a mile from the reception, after our wedding! We have nothing against the car, although perhaps we would have liked more space and provision for luggage. As soon as we put some luggage on the back the suspension bottoms, and the handling becomes diabolical.
G.A. What car will you buy next?
Mrs. R.J. If, and when, we start a family, then we will obviously replace the Mini, but I cannot see us selling the Seven for any reason whatsoever.
G.A. What Clubs do you belong to?
Robert We don't belong to any car clubs. Perhaps we ought to join Club Lotus but, you know what it's like, you never get round to this sort of thing ...
G.A. Has your car won any prizes?
Robert No. We don't compete with the vehicle in any four-wheel sporting events, and I have no plans to get into that scene.
G.A. Is your car in current daily use?
Robert No! We only use it for weekends, or if we both decide to take a day off on a Monday when the salon is closed.
G.A. What advice would you give to potential owners?
Robert I suppose you should buy the car from a reputable dealer and have it thoroughly checked out by a competent expert. I have met several unhappy owners, but this is usually because they bought a load of junk.
G.A. Any problems with parts?
Robert No. As we mentioned earlier, Chris Neils of Northwich seem to have everything.

P.O. is 26 and competed unsuccessfully for two years in Formula Ford before deciding to run a Lotus Seven in restricted events. He is a double-glazing salesman, and runs a Cortina out of his commission. He lives in Attleborough, Norfolk.

G.A. What made you first want a Lotus 7?
P.O. I went to school with lots of kids whose fathers worked at Lotus, and I think it was seeing Cox-Allinson's Black Brick Lotus Seven which really got me going after two years of getting nowhere in Formula Ford. I had done a Jim Russell course, but I just didn't have the money or the sponsorship to be competitive so I decided to prepare a Lotus Seven for sprints.
G.A. What repairs have been carried out?
P.O. Well, of course, the repairs have been as the result of over-exuberance, over-stress, over-driving. I am using a very strong Holbay engine, which has given no problems at all, along with a Lotus close-ratio gearbox. My main problems have been with brakes, chassis and suspension. I do all my own repairs, except engine and gearbox rebuilds, so cost is not a problem. I bent the chassis rather badly at the end of last season, but Midas Metalcraft at Staughton, near Bedford, completely re-jigged it for me at very reasonable cost.
G.A. What do you like most about the car?
P.O. The Lotus Seven has always been a thoroughly competitive concept and it is probably the nearest we will ever get to budget racing, as there will never be low-cost racing. As Colin Chapman was always the first to point out, you cannot put a touring chassis on the track without a mass of changes. I have had to do quite a lot of work in the dark and using other people's experience to make the car even halfway competitive. The biggest problem with the 7 is that like most Lotus cars it creates immediate animosity among the owners of those pseudo-performance sports cars based on the floorpan of production saloons. Let's be honest! The Austin-Healey and MG Midget are only Austin A35 convertibles and the MGB is an A60 convertible! Owners have always ganged up on the Seven, and it is to the eternal credit of Graham Nearn that he ran a compaign pointing out the stupidity of banning the 7 because it was literally "too fast to race".
G.A. What do you dislike about the car?
P.O. Whenever I find myself disliking the car I think of those horsemen who beat their horse because it fails a jump. If I am honest with myself, on those occasions when I have disliked the car I was really admitting my own failings. I am still trying to get on the first rung of the motor racing ladder with something like one-tenth of the budget available to those who finish ahead of me, but I've had my moments.!
G.A. What car will you buy next?
P.O. I have to give the whole Lotus Seven thing until the end of the season, and then probably give up racing unless somebody comes along and puts me in a works car. Then I will trade in my Cortina for a

Sierra and take up hang-gliding!
G.A. Have you ever won any trophies?
P.O. Yes! I have won my class on two occasions and enjoyed the fluke fortunes of a sprint F.T.D. because the skies opened and the rain came tumbling down just after my run at Goodwood. It was nice to have the trophy but I can never really take that much credit or pride. I have four small cups to show for two and a half seasons in a Seven. Perhaps it would have been cheaper to be a Walter Mitty and just buy a few and have them engraved
G.A. What advice would you give to potential owners?
P.O. Buy with your eyes wide open, buy in the anticipation that it is going to cost you a lot more than you intended up front because the car is very good, or after the purchase because it is ruddy awful! Of course, if you are going to buy for racing, get hold of the detailed regulations for every type of championship for which certain Sevens are eligible, and then buy a car that complies almost completely. I would buy a previous season's winning car.

BUYING

Buying a used Lotus 7 can be a frustrating activity because there are very few of these fine cars on the market at any one time. So, "First Find Your Seven" is an important factor. The timing of your Seven search is also quite important, and the Author recommends November, December, January and February: *not* the first sunny weekend in May! It will not be easy to find a wide choice of Sevens in the summer months, and a prospective buyer will need to study many motoring magazines and local papers before making his choice.

The main limitation, of course, will be the buyer's budget and this will dictate specification. It should be noted that some of the very early Series 1 cars are rare and can command prices higher than the Series 2. If the prospective buyer is considering the use of the car in serious motorsport, then he should check with Caterham Cars and the RAC Competitions Department to ensure that he purchases a vehicle with approximately the right specification and, where appropriate, year of registration. This applies particularly in the production classes, historic, post historic, etc.

When going to view a prospective Seven, one should ignore vehicles that have been fitted with very unusual engines, gearboxes and back axles, unless these are reasonably appropriate to the type – *ie* Fiat or Alfa Romeo 1600cc twin cam engines would not be too terrible, but many Seven lovers do not take too kindly to a 7-litre Oldsmobile V8 or Mazda Rotary! Having established the specification of the vehicle offered, obtain the registration number and approximate value and arrange with your Insurance Company temporary cover which will enable you to test drive the car.

Arriving to view the vehicle, stand well back and sight it from all angles to satisfy yourself that it looks conventional, that it is sitting square and level on the road and that it really is a Lotus or Caterham Seven. We make this last point because some specialist cars, and even that admirable little car the Dutton Phaeton, are sometimes advertised as "Lotus Seven-type" sports cars. To verify the vehicle's authenticity you will find a chassis plate under the bonnet which clearly says "Lotus Components Ltd". or "Caterham Cars Ltd".

Inspect the exterior of the vehicle more closely, especially the wing mountings, nose section, engine cover, etc. Make sure the windscreen is not cracked and that the hood and sidescreens are in good condition, especially if stowed away under the rear quarter tonneau.

The bonnet should be lifted off by two persons, especially in a high wind, taking great care not to scratch the headlights. It should then be placed where it cannot be blown over or trodden on as, after the windscreen, the bonnet seems to be one of the most vulnerable parts of the Seven. With the bonnet off, the complete engine gearbox and cooling system will be exposed to view and this can be given an external inspection, looking for oil leaks and signs of recent repairs, whilst obtaining a general impression of the level of maintenance and care which the vehicle has, or has not, enjoyed.

Take a close look at the chassis tubes and engine mountings to see if you can see cracks, 'tweaks' or signs of re-welding. Check that the rubber gaiters on the rack pinion are intact. Inspect the tyres and wheels for general condition and any signs of irregular wear.

Try to get the car on to a ramp for a full underside inspection, with particular attention to the gearbox mounting and rear axle location points, the trailing arms, the condition of the back axle casing and all rivets. The back axle casing has long been the traditional Achilles' heel of the Seven and profuse oil leakage is not uncommon. Once you are satisfied that the car is genuine, appears to be in good condition and that it is road-legal, a test drive is essential. For those who have never driven a Seven before, goggles should be worn by wearers of contact lenses or, at over 70 miles per hour, your lenses will be sucked from your eyes!

Having assured yourself that the brakes are in working order, start the car, noting whether the starter makes a normal noise or whether it sounds like a stone-crushing machine. Starter ring gear problems are well-known on the Seven, and although it is quite easy to take the engine out, such a requirement should be reflected in the price paid for the car.

If the car is fitted with Weber or Dellorto carburettors there is never any need to go looking for the choke. Just dab the accelerator a couple of times on a cold day, and away you go. Most of the noise comes out under the passenger's left elbow so exhaust noise will be fairly well masked. Then, once you really get your foot down, the induction roar adds to the cacophony of noise that *IS* the Seven – although later cars are much quieter, by law. It is hard to detect transmission noise with all the other distractions, but a keen ear should be able to hear a singing axle, or other unusual overtones. It is easy to look for too much smoke from the exhaust and overheating when on the move or in traffic.

Take the car up to its redline in the indirect gears and lift off in each gear in case she wants to tell you about a faulty gearbox. Handling should be reasonably good in a straight line, without too much hopping about. Over bumps, with two up, she may bottom a little and prove a little skittish on corners if you get the power on too soon in too big a dose. Brakes should be strong with reasonably heavy pedal pressure and rather unpredictable in the wet, but the car should not dart or dive under braking or acceleration. If in doubt, have a word with Club Lotus or Caterham Cars.

How much will you pay? Well, that varies as we mentioned earlier, but take a good look at advertised prices and always bid quite a bit lower to get the dealing started. However, remember that Sevens are in strong demand – and are priced accordingly.

Restoring a Seven

There are literally hundreds of people who are hoping to find an old and neglected Seven (or even a 6) parked in a barn. Occasionally one such car is located and the other searchers redouble their efforts ...

The actual restoration of a Seven can be troublesome if the aluminium panels have to be removed from the chassis frame to replace bent or rusted tubes, or because the aluminium has at last crumbled away due to electrolytic corrosion. There *are* specialists who can straighten a bent chassis, but a completely new replacement is the best investment for a long term restoration. Almost all the other parts are still available from Ford and other manufacturers with the exception of the Triumph Pennant axle, although these do turn up in scrap yards. Ford-engined cars can of course benefit from a "factory exchange unit", except the original 1172 side valve.

Many restoration projects come to a halt after an energetic disassembly job. It is better to rebuild a complete car that has been stored following MOT failure, than to take delivery of a chassis and boxes of assorted bits and pieces. "Basket cases" as they are called among restorers, cause more headaches and overdrafts than complete cars – so beware!

YOU CAN'T REGISTER A REBUILT SEVEN WITHOUT A LOG BOOK OR REGISTRATION DOCUMENT AND A CHASSIS PLATE. From time to time, enthusiasts obtain an old Seven chassis and set about building a Seven of their own. When they come to register the car as a Lotus Seven the authorities in Great Britain will only permit this if the appropriate documents exist and can be produced. Otherwise the car will receive a Q-plate and be registered as a "Special".

Racing Sevens

Racing Sevens and Sevens that have been raced (and there is a big difference) can usually be detected by the bunches of scrutineers' labels tied to the steering column plus a larger than life roll-over hoop. Such additions as oil coolers, wider wheels, air dams and wings can also give the game away. A successful racing Seven will be offered as such, but if an owner has dabbled with the odd competitive event and found himself *and* the car uncompetitive, then probably there is no harm done. Just check that the chassis is straight and the oil pressure healthy.

If your proposed purchase has been raced seriously by its present or previous owner, that might not be a bad thing: assuming the car was tended by a skilled mechanic and prepared professionally. A car that has competed, with tender loving care between races, can be in better condition than an average 'used at weekends only' Seven. The worst buy would be a Seven that has been used for occasional sprints or club races without the benefit of professional preparation. That car could have an overstressed crankshaft, fatigued first gear and a back axle that is about to cry 'enough'. A well-prepared car can declare its history via up-market shock absorbers *ie* Koni, Bilstein or Sachs, competition brake pads and linings, an oil cooler and Aeroquip brake and fuel lines, plus a top quality rollover bar and full-harness safety belts. Although it may be presented for sale standing on ordinary steel wheels and 'nothing-special' tyres a top class set of alloys shod with Goodyear NCTs or Pirelli P7s might be thrown in to sweeten the deal – then you'll know – but so what?

If a Seven has been raced some of the components, as mentioned earlier, may have reached the end of their working life earlier than would otherwise be expected. The most expensive mistake is to buy a Seven with a bent chassis as this will need replacement or expensive rejigging. As the multitubular design of the chassis makes it difficult to detect distortion your prospective purchase should be subjected to several tests to ensure that you are not about to buy trouble. An alignment check front *and* rear is a good starting point, after you have run your hand over the tyres to see (or feel) if there is any 'feathering' to indicate unusual and excessive toe-out or toe-in. If the tyres are new this test is, of course, invalid. Measure the distance between wheel centres on each side of the car to + or – 1/10th of an inch, then carry out the 'chalked string' test. Mike Walters, Lotus' Chief Quality Engineer was famous for saying in his Northern drawl: 'There's nought as straight as a tight piece of string' and he was, and still is, 100% right. Drop a bob weight from four or more fixed points on the car, *ie* shock absorber bottom mounting points and mark the position in chalk on a flat garage or workshop floor. Now stretch chalked string from one point to its diagonal opposite and 'twang' the string as it lies tight across the floor. This will leave a fine chalk line. Now repeat the operation until you have one or more central crossing points. These should a) be in line and b) mirror equal when it comes to dimensions from the outer perimeter defined by wheel centres, etc. Such a system eliminates the car that has been made to track correctly by the use of a heavy hammer and some chassis paint! The author has stressed this business of chassis integrity as this can cause the most trouble and expense in Seven ownership. You may have to rebuild an engine, fit new parts in the gearbox or back axle, but these are not as annoying in time (or money consuming) as a chassis replacement or stripdown for rejigging.

The definitive Lotus Seven

A purist Seven lover would have to chose an immaculate, and original, 1963 or 1964 Super Seven "Cosworth" with a close-ratio gearbox. This car represented what was probably the best balance of all Lotus Seven virtues, being light, swift and the most fun to drive.

Perhaps the buyer would be permitted three non-standard additions: disc brakes on the front, radial tyres *and* a fuel gauge! A Kenlow fan would also be specified.

The Ford 1340cc had the 3-bearing crank, and was an over square engine. Features included raised compression, Cosworth cam, twin Weber 40DCOE carburettors and a four branch exhaust. The result was around 95bhp at 6250rpm: enough power to really spin the wheels away from a standing start leaving yards of black, burning rubber in the car's wake.

The 1340cc Cosworth Seven was the nearest thing to racing car performance to be found in a genuine road car. It might only have had a top speed of a shade over 100, but 95bhp in a car weighing less than 10cwt is still a potent formula for fast driving, even today.

CLUBS, SPECIALISTS & BOOKS

Clubs

There are two national clubs in the UK which are an obvious choice for Seven owners.

Club Lotus, with over 3500 Lotus-owning members, offers a wide variety of benefits and activities to its members including D.I.Y. repair seminars, special insurance, track test days, concours d'elegance, area meetings, Grand Prix visits etc. Club Lotus can also put owners in touch with Lotus clubs in many countries throughout the world.

PO Box 8, Dereham, Norfolk, England. (0362 4459).

Lotus Seven Club. Based at Caterham Cars HQ at Caterham, the club brings together Seven owners throughout the United Kingdom and, although most of the activities are centred in the south, a northern group has now been launched. An annual rally is also held.

Caterham Cars Ltd., Seven House, 36/40 Tower End, Caterham Hill, Surrey, England (0883 46666).

Wales & West of England 7 Owners Club, 5 Bamber House, Plantation Drive, Croesyceiliog, Cwmbran, Gwent.

Lotus Limited, PO Box L, College Park, Maryland, USA.

Club Lotus Australia. 40 Bellambi Street, Northbridge, New South Wales.

Lotus Seven Club Germany, Niederkasselerstrasse 18, 400 Dusseldorf II, West Germany.

Specialists

Caterham Cars Limited, Seven House, Town End, Caterham Hill, Surrey, England (0883 42382/42381/46666) are the obvious first choice for Lotus Seven parts.

Chris Smith, 13 Primrose Hill, Ind Est., Netherton, Dudley, W. Midlands, England. (0384 234788) is a specialist in the restoration of the Lotus 6 and Seven as well as manufacturer of the Westfield replica of the Lotus Eleven and Seven Mk I Replicas.

Vegantune Limited. Cradge Bank, Spalding, Lincs, England (0775 4846). Suppliers of Twin Cam engines to Caterham; also Lotus restoration specialists since 1964.

Books

Legend of the Lotus Seven by Dennis Ortenberger. Osprey.
Lotus Seven Workshop Manual. Caterham Cars Limited.
Lotus Seven 1957-1980 and **Lotus Seven Collection No. 1** Brooklands Books.
Lotus by Chris Harvey. Osprey.
Lotus: The First Ten Years by Ian Smith. Motor Racing Publications.
The Story of Lotus 1961-1971 by Doug Nye. Motor Racing Publications. 28 Devonshire Road, London W.4 2HD.
LOTUS – The Complete Story by Chris Harvey. Haynes Publishing Group.
The Lotus Seven Buyer's Pocket Book by Graham Arnold. Club Lotus Publications.

PHOTO GALLERY

1. *A very rare 'Boat-tailed' Lotus Seven Series 1. Note the registration.*

2. *Patrick McGoohan (L) and Graham Nearn (R) with the Lotus Seven featured in the famous TV series "The Prisoner". Note the Elan wheels.*

1

2

3

4

6. Caterham Car's 'Production Line!' (Thoroughbred & Classic Car)

7. A 1983 Caterham with its snug weather protection and all-round visibility. (Thoroughbred & Classic Car)

8. Super Seven A (A is for Avon). Car by Caterham, cosmetics by Avon coachworks. Note quarter flyscreens, spare wheel cover and those ultra modern wheels.

5

3. A hillclimb Seven 1600 with non-standard air intake. (Jim Penson)

4. The first production Seven Series 4 at Hethel in 1970.

5. Series 4 cockpit. Note comprehensive dials, rocker switches and moulded dash.

6

7

8

9

10

9. *Putting the clock back? The Caterham Seven for Germany features cycle-type wings as on the Series 1 Lotus Seven.*

10. *The 'long cockpit' Caterham Lotus Seven.*

11. *'Winged Chariot'. A German modified Seven with picnic tray rear wing to keep rain off the luggage! (Richard Spelberg)*

12. *Caterham/Vegantune belt-driven 140bhp Twin Cam engine.*

13. *The Seven Twin Cam legend lives on. Vegantune's Twin Cam engine (VTA) ready for fitment to the Twin Cam Caterham Seven.*

11

12

13

14

15

14. The ultimate 'Black Brick'. Note the side pods and top vented nose section. (Duncan P. Hands)

15. Black Brick and Cox-Allison put the power down. (Duncan P. Hands)

16. Chris Smith in his Lotus Six at Donington in 1979. Chris is now building a Mk I replica. (Jim Evans)

17-23. Wheel fashion changes. (17) is the standard steel wheel on a Series 4. (18) Elan 13 inch wheels update a 7A Series 1. (19) 'Brand Lotus' alloy wheels by GKN, circa 1970-71. (20) Caterham's alloy choice. (21) Cosmic wheels. (22 & 23) Variations on a theme; the spider's web.

16

17

18

19

20

21

22

23

24

24. *Original 2-into-1 GN silencer – unpopular with pedestrians!*

25

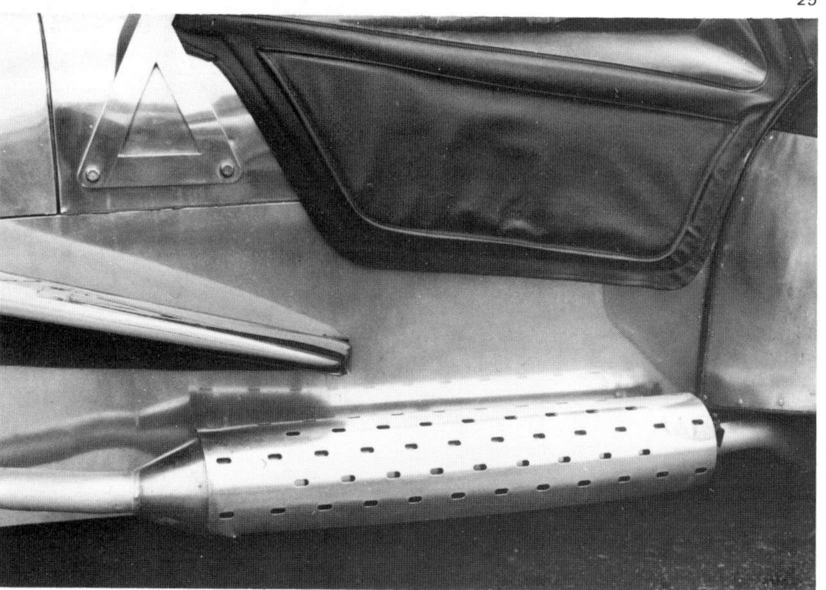

26

25. *Universal one-piece windscreen fixing, complete with pre-war style tax-disc holder.*

26. *Passenger's elbow and ankle protection, seen on a Series 3. Only a car as low as the Lotus Seven could provide, in the same component, protection to such diverse parts of the anatomy!*

27. *Non-standard chromed protector, looking suspiciously like part of a redundant bumper bar.*

28. *Legal limit? A larger than standard silencer, but is it quieter?*

27

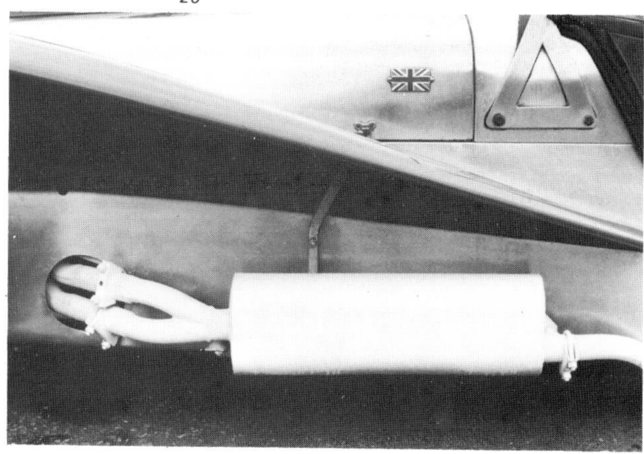

28

29

30

31

32

33

34

29-33. Bonnet architecture. (29) Power bulge conceals a downdraught carburettor on a Ford pushrod engine. (30) Ram-air, forward facing scoop feeding twin Webers on a Series 2. (31) Another pushrod Ford, this time fitted with twin Webers breathing through individual bell-mouths. (32 & 33) Two versions of pancake-type airfilters fitted to twin 40 DCOE Webers. The latter still has the power bulge used in earlier, downdraught installations.

34. A good view of the steeply inclined coil spring/damper unit as pioneered on the Lotus Six.

35

36

37

38

39

35. *Typical Chapman-style suspension. It's not as fragile as it looks.*

36. *There was little change over the years; compare this cycle wing Series 1 with the prevous photograph of a much later model.*

37. *Beautifully executed, but non-standard, fully-adjustable, double-wishbone, Rose-jointed front suspension.*

38. *A one-off British-installed 907 Lotus 16-valve, 2-litre unit. A turbo version is in the making!*

39. *No space to spare in this big-valve Twin Cam from Caterham.*

40. *Twin SUs and a 3-branch exhaust system pep up the 7A.*

40

41

41. Twin Cam sprint car. Note radiator and oil-cooler and cylinder head stiffening.

42. Inelegant perhaps, but secure. The finger nail-breaking head studs on the screen frame.

43. A full length tonneau on a Series 1.

44. Flexible side screen as offered on the Series 1, 2 & 3. The bottom section hinges horizontally to encourage 'Lotus Elbow' (see text).

45. A real improvement in all-weather equipment. The draught-proof head and rigid side screens of the Series 4.

42

43

44

45

46

47

48

46 & 47. Putting the hood up is easy for two people, or even single-handed but ...

48. ... entering is a knack!

49. Caterham's improved three-quarter vision, hood.

50. Rear wings without stoneguards invite stone chips. This wing is obviously lately repainted.

51. The essential small stoneguard.

49

50

51

52

53

54

52. Attractive pre-war style torpedo side-lights, seen here with matching chrome headlamps.

53. The cycle-type wing of the Series 1 gave way to ...

54. ... the American-inspired 'clam-shell' type, supposedly to improve the styling.

55

56

55. *A Series 1 with its number plate in the original, but now illegal, position.*

56. *A Series 2 with the less attractively-positioned, but legal, number plate.*

57 & 58. *A Series 4 showing its more integrated styling and 'squarer' line.*

57

58

59

59. *The clean cam-tail of the Series 4: blunt but aerodynamic.*

60 & 61. *This heavily modified Caterham Seven, in both performance and looks is just plain mean!*

62. *Uncluttered simplicity. This dash has the essential easy-to-view instruments ideal for road or track.*

63. *Neat, standard, twin wipers. On the Series 1 they were extras!*

60

61

62

63

64

65

66

67

64 & 65. *Lotus line-ups at the 1983 meeting at the National Motor Museum, Beaulieu.*

66 & 67. *There's nothing that cannot be done to a Lotus Seven, provided you are determined enough.*

68. *Lotus Eater.*

68

C1

C2

C1. Sisters under the skin. The XI came before the Seven, but they have a lot in common (see text).

C2. Series 1. Note the tall 15 inch wheels and narrow tyres.

C3

C4

C3. *Concours condition ... Series 2 in perfect state.*

C4. *Series 3 Seven. Spot the differences between this and the red S2.*

C5

C6

C5. Series 4 with proprietary cast wheels which are not really in tune with the styling.

C6. 'AOK' is the number and describes this S4 perfectly. Note owner's choice of wheels.

C7

C8

C7. This German Seven says 'GO', and has custom wheels and non-standard air intake bulge.

C8. Cover girl. One of the world's fastest Sevens (see text).

C9

C10

C11

C12

C9. Too fast to race?

C10. The genuine Lotus badge with Chapman's initials. This will soon be dropped by Lotus.

C11. Caterham's proud symbol of Twin Cam power

C12. The badge that many Caterham owners take off – to fit a Lotus original.

C13

C14

C13. All that spare space in the engine bay! BMC A-Series-powered Series 1.

C14. Cosworth power, combined with braking of racing specification.

C15

C15. Show finish big valve Twin Cam Caterham. Note tight fit under nose cone also pancake air cleaner/silencers.

C16. A German Seven with Ford BDA power.

C17. "One man's meat is another man's poison!" Rover 3.5-litre V8 engine in a Series 4 custom Seven.

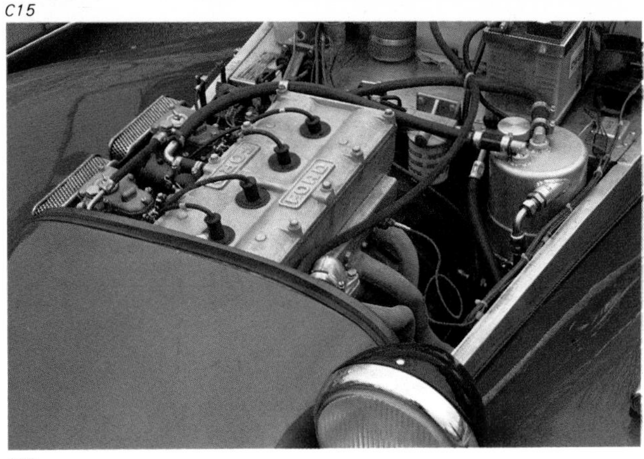

C16

C17

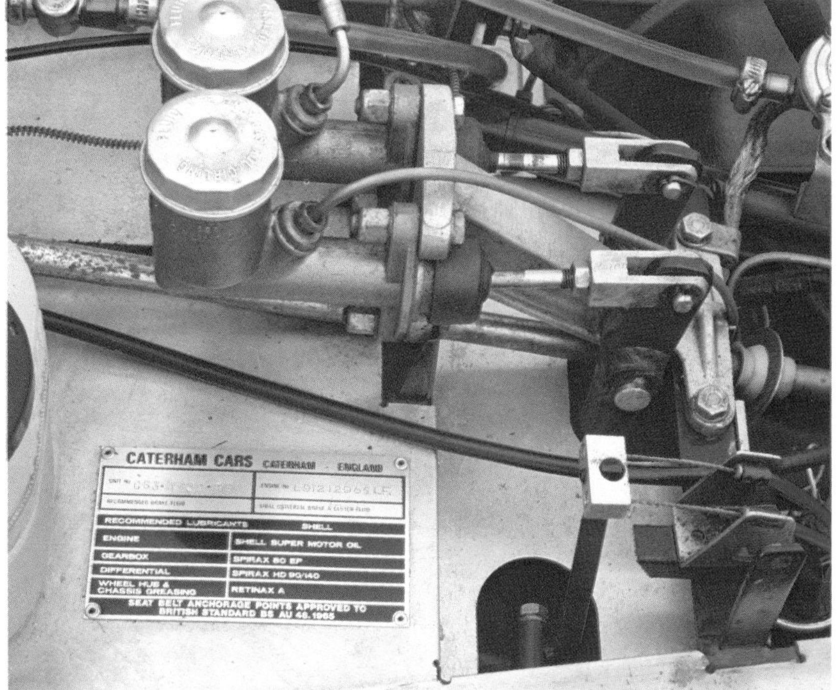

C18

C18. Caterham chassis plate. Lotus-built cars said: "Lotus Components Limited".

C19. Full house facia and exotic trimming. Every possible instrument and switch, all fitted in a confined space.

C20. We've heard of gold plated bath taps, but ...!

C20

C19